12-99

ʌ is to
dat.

E.20A

30130504087662

STL

371.37
DIL
c/R

USING DISCUSSION IN CLASSROOMS

USING DISCUSSION
IN CLASSROOMS

James T. Dillon

Open University Press
Buckingham · Philadelphia

Open University Press
Celtic Court
22 Ballmoor
Buckingham
MK18 1XW

and
1900 Frost Road, Suite 101
Bristol, PA 19007, USA

First Published 1994
Reprinted 1995

A catalogue record of this book is available from the British Library

ISBN 0 335 19324 2 (pbk)   ISBN 0 335 19325 0 (hbk)

Library of Congress Cataloging-in-Publication Data

Dillon, J. T.
  Using discussion in classrooms / James T. Dillon.
    p. cm.
  Includes bibliographical references and index.
  ISBN 0–335–19325–0   ISBN 0–335–19324–2 (pbk)
  1. Forums (Discussion and debate)   I. Title.
LC6515.D55   1994
371.3'7–dc20   94–11822
                                                         CIP

Typeset by Vision Typesetting, Manchester
Printed and bound in Great Britain by
Biddles Ltd, Guildford and King's Lynn

CONTENTS

THE PRACTICE
OF DISCUSSION

Through discussion we join with others in forming answers to our questions about what to think and how to act. We also use discussion to form our young. It is an ancient and essential educative activity that is rarely practised in schools.

How might discussion be rightly practised in classrooms? In addressing this question, this book displays all the principal things to know about discussion. Each chapter answers one fundamental question about one fundamental thing (along with subsidiary questions about aspects of that thing). In all, only six things are involved. The first and last things to know about discussion are its *nature* and *rationale*: What is it? (Chapter 1) and Why use it? (Chapter 6). In between are the four other principal things that together make a discussion: a *subject* or topic suitable for discussion; *people* disposed to discuss it; and certain *behaviours* and *language* appropriate to discussion. That is: What things are discussed? (Chapter 2), Who engages in discussion? (Chapter 3), How to conduct a discussion? (Chapter 4) and How to talk in discussion? (Chapter 5).

As additional help to learning these things about discussion, other materials are supplied at the end of the book. The variety of materials helps for study, analysis and practise of discussion. The *bibliography* gives a select guide to further study of discussion in its various respects and through various kinds of literature. Readers may select from among (1) general treatments of the concept and pedagogy of discussion, (2) anthologies on discussion, (3) studies on discussion in the various subject-matter areas, (4) source materials from research reviews and bibliographies on discussion, and (5) textbooks on discussion in general.

The *transcripts* are five verbatim records of actual classroom exchanges. The first two supply contrasting examples of recitation and discussion. The other three represent contrasting examples of discussion. These transcripts provide real-life illustrations of the points made throughout the chapters, and they may be used by the reader to analyse in detail for selected aspects of interest. For instance, the reader might look through the transcripts for some principle of discussion at work, or for certain ways of talking that are conducive to discussion.

The *exercises* are not for reading or for analysis but for practice and action. They suggest several dozen useful ways that a reader might act on various points and might practise certain aspects of discussion. For instance, they suggest practising specific ways of talking that help a class to discuss. With good fortune a reader may join with others in doing these exercises or at least in sharing the individual effort, as in a course or programme on discussion. But the exercises may also be done alone, and apart from a classroom as well as within a teaching situation.

By engaging our young in discussion, we induce them into present goods and conjoin them with ancient and modern exemplars in the ongoing practice of human community and inquiry. Discussion has an ancient tradition, yet we know little of its history and we can never be certain of its prospects. The tradition is fragile and impossible to trace along any direct or developmental line. We can, however, savour its greatest sources and invoke them to sustain us in our efforts to discuss.

These sources of discussion count first the example of Socrates in fifth-century B.C. Greece, in his dialogues as recounted by Plato and Xenophon. We have as well the deliberations by Athenians of Socrates' time, recounted in the histories of Thucydides and Xenophon, and the orations of Demosthenes. From there we look for hints to first-century A.D. Rome and the *Discourses* of

Musonius Rufus, and to twelfth-century Paris for the dialectician Peter Abelard in his *Sic et Non*.

The rest of the tradition comes to us in the main through England and liberal political theory. We refer to Francis Bacon in the sixteenth century, less for his famous writings on scientific method than for his quiet practices of deliberation in nascent Parliamentary committees. Even more we refer to John Stuart Mill's manifesto *On Liberty* in 1859, and to John Dewey's corpus of writing on group participation in democratic society, as in *Democracy and Education* in 1916.

In the 1930s, we see courses and textbooks on discussion, and the practise of it throughout entire curricula in select American universities, part of a recovery of ancient rhetoric and then of dialectic (perhaps in response to Soviet Marxist dialectic?). The Second World War era in the USA and Anglo-Saxon countries saw a vast and intensified striving for discussion as a means of democratic decision making, or at least involvement, poignantly revealed in books such as Bruno Lasker's *Democracy through Discussion* in 1949, and in innumerable discussion groups even in the armed forces and war industries (to war's end, only), in radio and TV panels with their listeners' groups, in all manner of citizen and community organizations, in book clubs, unions, business, religion, police and social work, psychotherapy and adult education. And the schools?

In a symposium in 1954, a professor rehearsed the marvels of discussion, proclaimed it of unrivalled efficacy for educating the hearts and minds of students, and concluded with this prophesy: 'I also prophesy that the years ahead will see a rapid and impressive extension of the discussion method throughout our land.' As for discussion in schools, nothing much is known to have happened, for example, more discussion in classrooms. But the intellectual and moral tradition of discussion and the passion for its practise in schools were fully recovered and moreover given original contemporary impulse by David Bridges in his *Education, Democracy and Discussion* in 1979. Behind his stance we see marshalled the whole of English liberal political democracy, and Dewey as well, with epistemological grounds stretching clearly all the way back to Socrates. Recently joining us to this tradition is a work of practice as well as reflection, *Turning the Soul* (by Sophie Haroutunian-Gordon in 1991), referring today's American inner-city schools to Plato, if not Socrates, via teenaged discussion of a play by the Englishman Bacon's contemporary, Shakespeare.

Other educational researchers, too, have lately been working in this tradition, as seen by the scholars from various disciplines and countries who have contributed to the anthologies, *Questioning and Discussion* in 1988 and *Deliberation in Education and Society* in 1994 (both edited by J.T. Dillon), and *Teaching and Learning through Discussion* in 1990 (edited by W. Wilen). This present book also joins in the tradition, adducing experience, theory and research to the right practise of discussion in classrooms.

Each one of us lives this tradition when we join in discussion with our fellows and our children. There is nothing at all fancy about discussion. It is a fundamental human relation and essential educative activity. Nothing about it is beyond ordinary teachers and pupils in everyday classrooms. It requires of us no special skills and circumstances. Discussion is well within our reach. If we are willing, we too can practise discussion rightly.

To practise discussion rightly, we will in the end need to know its rationale, or why we use it – along with what things are discussed, who the people are that discuss these things, and how to act and to talk in discussion. But first we need to know the nature of discussion. So we begin by asking, what is it?

1

WHAT IS DISCUSSION?

When we ask about the nature of discussion, we want to know its essence and distinctiveness. What, at bottom, is discussion? How is it different from other kinds of group talk? We can isolate the essence of discussion through definition and analysis of its principles. We can locate its distinctiveness through contrast of its characteristics with those of everyday discourse and especially classroom recitation. In that way, we come to discover that discussion is a unique form of group interaction, where people join together in addressing some question of common concern, something they need to understand, appreciate or decide.

Knowing the nature of discussion is almost enough to make us long to engage in it as an essential educative and human activity. If only we knew how to do it and had what it takes! But that will be for the later chapters to discover. Right now we have to find out what it is.

ESSENCE OF DISCUSSION

What, at bottom, is discussion? Before giving a definition and identifying the principles of discussion, we need to consider how the term is used.

Terms

The terms of discussion are commonly confused both in academic and everyday discourse. Educators, like other people, use the term in two ways: as a rubric covering all manner of back-and-forth talk or interaction, and as a designator of one distinct form of back-and-forth talk. Here in this book 'discussion' will be used in the second way.

In the first usage, as a rubric or umbrella term, discussion covers an ill-defined range of talk. It embraces exchanges otherwise termed conversation, argument, debate, bull session and recitation, and it stretches to include interview and negotiation. It even describes talk that apparently is no exchange at all, such as lecture ('I will now discuss . . .'); exchanges that are not talk, such as a person deliberating within self; and activity that is neither talk nor exchange, such as an author writing a treatment of some issue. In this book, 'discussion' refers to group interaction only, oral exchanges between two or more people.

Even when limited to group interaction, discussion is scarcely a narrow term. It is confusingly used to denote any number and variety of exchanges. The confusion can be entertaining. For instance, an article on discussion in teaching bears the title of conversation (Greene 1954), while a book entitled teaching through conversation (Haroutunian-Gordon 1991) bears on discussion, and another book entitled discussion (Johnson 1979) bears on recitation. A study on recitation (Stodolsky *et al.* 1981) distinguishes it from discussion and reports data on each; a study of classroom processes (Goodlad 1984) does not distinguish discussion from recitation but reports data for everything lumped as discussion. Finally, a book on using discussion (VanMents 1990) lists a dozen forms of discussion, including debate, panel, forum, buzz group and peer tutoring but not conversation or recitation.

As we see, educators (and not us alone) find ourselves in a real mix-up, and we need first of all to recognize this confusion of terms so that we can straighten out what we are doing or at least talking about when we use 'discussion'. Second, we would be wrong to treat this matter as a mere question of semantics, and we would not find it useful to define away the confusion of terms by stipulation. What is important is to keep clear the thing to which reference is being made. On this point it becomes easy to distinguish discussion from other forms of group interaction – just as these other forms are easily distinguished one from another.

In this book, the term discussion will apply not to a range of classroom interaction but to one particular activity. It is used not as a rubric to cover various exchanges but as a designator of a specific type of exchange. It does not, for example, refer to those exchanges which are otherwise called recitation, bull session, conversation, debate, argument, guided inquiry, Socratic method, and so on. All of these are also commonly called by an additional term, discussion. But the one type of group interaction here referred to by 'discussion' is not commonly called by any other name. For instance, recitation is commonly also called discussion, whereas the interaction here termed discussion is never called recitation. Discussion has no other proper name.

In this book, therefore, discussion should be understood first of all as *not* recitation, conversation and the rest. It refers to one distinct form of group interaction. What is that?

Definition

Discussion is a form of group interaction, people talking back-and-forth with one another. What they talk about is an issue, some topic that is in question for them. Their talk consists of advancing and examining different proposals over the issue. The proposals may be various understandings, facts, suggestions, opinions, perspectives, experiences and the like. These are examined for their contribution towards resolving the issue.

As people talk and relate in this way, they begin to form together new, more satisfying answers to their question. For instance, they come to a better understanding, a new appreciation, a wiser judgement, a firmer resolve. The kind of thing that counts as an answer depends on the matter in question and on the question about that matter. If the question concerns what to think about something, for example, the answer might be some knowledge or understanding; if the question concerns how to act, the answer might be some judgement or resolve. If these are not in question, there can be no answer and there will be no discussion. People do not discuss a topic that they already know and understand – that matter is closed, it is not an issue for them. They do not discuss actions that they are resolved to undertake – that matter is decided, their minds are made up. Similarly, people do not discuss experiences whose meaning is plain to them, nor their indisputable feelings or incontestable values. When they do discuss these things they have some question about them and they join with others to form an answer.

Discussion is group address to a question in common. People resolve together some question at issue for them, something they need to understand, appreciate or decide. Since it is their question and they need a good answer to it, they want to hear divergent views on the matter and they are willing to change their view for a better one, after scrutinizing all proposals as alternative candidates for answering their question in some way satisfying to them. The people do this together, in communal address to the question, in mutuality and concert of effort, in reciprocal exchange of opinion and influence, forming their ideas, sentiments and decisions over the matter at issue.

Discussion is a particular form of group interaction where members join together in addressing a question of common concern, exchanging and examining different views to form their answer, enhancing their knowledge or understanding, their appreciation or judgement, their decision, resolution or action over the matter at issue.

Principles

Principles are the constitutive elements of discussion, those things that make discussion what it is. All of them may be found in the definition of discussion. Only a few are mentioned explicitly; the rest are implications, presuppositions, elaborations of the points mentioned.

The most comprehensive and detailed set of principles has been identified by the English philosopher and educator, David Bridges (1979, 1988, 1990). They may strike us as terribly rational or intellectual points. Indeed, they have been derived through a philosophical method of conceptual analysis and they bear particularly on discussion as a classical means of pursuing intellectual inquiry. But these principles are also inspired by the tradition of liberal democratic political theory and they are pointed at the practice of education.

What conditions have to be met in order for us to say that people are engaged in a discussion of some subject matter? Bridges answers with a series of conditions that are logical, moral and intellectual, together with a further mixed set describing the openness of discussion. These principles will give us more than enough ideas as to the essence of discussion.

Logical conditions

It would not make sense for us to say that people were discussing something if, for example, they were not talking with one another or if they were all holding forth the same view of the matter. The five logical conditions are quite basic. They hold that for discussion people must talk to one another, listen to one another, and respond to one another. When they talk, moreover, they must severally be putting forward more than one point of view on the subject, and they must be intending to develop their understanding of the topic, their knowledge and/or judgement regarding the matter under discussion.

Classroom interaction that satisfies these conditions can be said to be discussion – to that extent. Without these in some degree, the interaction must be something else and not discussion. From a developmental point of view, a class might meet these conditions to progressively greater extent. For instance, more students talk in the discussion and students talk more; students listen more carefully and over more extended time; their contributions are more responsive to what others are saying, and more frequently related to the preceding contribution; they are more purposeful in talking for understanding the topic under discussion.

Moral dispositions

These are principles of conduct that are presupposed in the logical conditions. They form the moral culture of the social group in discussion. Students and teacher must share these six assumptions to some extent, otherwise they cannot discuss together.

1 *Reasonableness*. The discussants are willing to listen to reason, to accommodate interests and views on the evidence. They are not dogmatic, immovably convinced of their own opinion, unamenable to the influence of reasons, evidence, argument.

2 *Peaceableness* and *orderliness*. They observe rules that facilitate the exchange, such as 'one speaker at a time'. They do not interrupt or shout down opinions they dislike.

3 *Truthfulness*. They deliberately speak what they believe to be true and they will not speak deliberate untruth. They are not silent, reticent or covert.

4 *Freedom*. People are not prevented from offering their opinion. They are not subject to restraints, not afraid to speak freely and sincerely because of ridicule or embarrassment.

5 *Equality*. People have presumptive regard for the interests and opinions of each participant. They do not feel that for some reason it would be improper for this or that participant to express a personal opinion.

6 *Respect for persons*. Participants share a measure of reciprocal regard, some relation of humanity and caring. They do not desire or act to make someone's opinion prevail at all costs over others.

Intellectual qualities

The first two intellectual qualities are epistemological foundations of discussion, reflecting a special attitude or stance towards knowledge and authority. The other eight qualities concern especially the cultivation of understanding in discussion, four of them describing the enrichment of understanding and four the refinement of understanding of the topic. Students and teacher exhibit these attitudes and concerns as they discuss, they grow in these qualities and they press others to exhibit them as well.

1 *Respect for opinions of others*: discussants can expect respectful attention and accept to give it.

2 *Scepticism of authority*: authority (including one's own) as uncertain or corrigible; knowledge and beliefs as contestable or dubitable; caution in accepting another's say-so.

3 *Diversity*: concern that an appropriate variety of perspectives is made available to the group.
4 *Responsiveness*: concern that students are sensitive, appreciative and open-minded in response to the opinions of others.
5 *Judiciousness*: concern that students give proper hearing to views, and not accept or reject views arbitrarily.
6 *Reflectiveness*: concern that students should be thoughtful, reflective and searching in their self-awareness.
7 *Evidence*: concern for reasons, evidence and argument.
8 *Clarity*: concern for clarity and precision in the expression of meaning, so that others can understand the contribution.
9 *Conciseness*: expressing substance in the minimum of words.
10 *Consistency*: concern for coherence, consistency and consecutiveness in thought and argument.

Openness dimensions

Openness is a precondition of discussion. It describes the absence of restraint on the development of understanding and judgement over the topic under discussion. To the extent that group interaction is closed, understanding cannot develop and the activity is not discussion. All possible aspects of discussion must be open, or at least not closed in principle.

1 The subject matter is open for discussion.
2 The participants are open-minded.
3 The discussion is open to all contributions – all arguments, evidence, points of view, criticism.
4 The discussion is open to all persons. Good reason has to be shown for excluding anyone.
5 The time-limit is open. It is not closed. The discussion is not prematurely rushed to conclusion, and not scheduled for an impossibly short time.
6 The outcomes are open. The conclusion is not predictable, not pre-specified or pre-determined.
7 The purposes and practices are overt.
8 The discussion is open-ended. There is no requirement that the discussion come to a single conclusion; it may come to various conclusions or come to no conclusion at all.

Phenomenological elements

These principles describe the consciousness of participants in a discussion. They are identified by the English educator R.W.K. Paterson (1970) through a philosophical analysis of discussion from the perspective of existential phenomenology. What is the state of consciousness of any class in which the conditions for genuine discussion are being met? Paterson answers that they are experiencing free mutual address and intending a common search for meaning:

1 *Freedom of address.* Every participant is conscious of a freedom to address anyone in the class on any occasion, and this freedom is recognized by all other participants. Discussion is an activity of mutual address in a class setting that invites completely free and open exchanges.

2 *Search for meaning.* Participants are consciously intending a common search for meaning. To discuss something is to ask one another, 'What does it mean?' In their exchanges, participants bear witness to the meaning of the subject in their understanding and life, and they invite the others to share this construal of experience; they listen and enter into the other's world as it is being articulated over the subject being discussed.

Both of these principles entail togetherness (mutual address, common search). They make plain to us, in case we have not noticed so far, that discussion engages us as persons in relation to other persons. This matter is of the *essence* of discussion. Talk alone is not the essence of discussion. Discussion is not just talk but interaction, and it is group interaction. The interaction is not just an intellectual exchange of minds but a social, moral, emotional, personal interrelation. It is a relation in which, as suggested by our definition of discussion, we join with others in addressing our questions of common concern. On that note, perhaps we could usefully pause to review the principles just set out here, now with an eye to appreciating the meanings that they might connote other than the verbal and intellectual.

Listed this way one after another, these many principles may look daunting and perhaps tiresome and picky. Indeed, they do pick apart the essence of discussion, specifying in detail the various things that make discussion what it is. We might select one or another set of these principles for special attention as we may find useful. They can do two things for us. First, these principles can give us knowledge and some understanding and appreciation of the essence of discussion. That befits the topic of this part of the chapter. Second, these principles can help us to analyse classroom interaction to tell whether and wherein it is a discussion. Later in this chapter we will return to these principles to display the difference between discussion and recitation. That will be one means for us to grasp the distinctiveness of discussion.

DISTINCTIVENESS OF DISCUSSION

What is discussion like by contrast to other forms of group talk? Discussion is plainly different from the talk in right-answer recitation, opinion-venting bull sessions, position-defending and victory-seeking debates and arguments, and the aimless wandering and carefree chatter of conversation. The classroom favourite among these is recitation. But in classrooms we can also hear the other forms of interaction which are common in everyday discourse.

Everyday discourse

Conversation differs from discussion in every respect save that people are talking back and forth. The topic of conversation changes as people want now to talk about one thing, next about another; the talk shifts from topic to topic, whereas in discussion the talk concentrates upon one topic which is maintained, extended or developed. In conversations, anyone can speak about nearly anything they wish; they don't have to address either the current topic or the previous speaker; and they needn't even listen to the previous exchange but only await their chance to enter in – and not wait too long, for someone may start a new turn at talk as soon as the speaking party hesitates for a word or pauses to draw a breath. Conversations start and finish by happenstance, ending, for instance, when interest is exhausted or attention is distracted. Discussion is disciplined and concerted talk by contrast to the carefree interludes of conversational exchange. And that is part of the attraction of conversation. It is an aimless and effortless way of talking together, requiring next to nothing of us by way of commitment while giving us in return a pleasant way of passing the time. Discussion is not a pastime.

Arguments and debates are more effortful and sustained than conversations, yet they remain distinct from discussion. They begin with pre-formed opinions and proceed to defend them one against the other, in a contesting exchange ending in victory for one side, or in a stand-off where the two sides maintain their distance unaffected by each other. In discussion, the positions are formed during the process and they are positions in common; they are cooperatively developed, partly through the perception and adoption of other people's views, which are adjudged for their merits in relation to the question at issue rather than the person who holds and presents them. Moreover, in discussion it is never a matter of two sides. There are multiple proposals and the one finally developed and settled upon is rarely one of the opinions put forward during the earlier stages of discussion. It is a new position, not an old one. And it is not the position of any one speaker but of the group. It is, so to speak, ours, not one of ours. The resolution in discussion is neither one of the sides as in an argument or debate: it is a new side, our side.

Bull sessions are a form of everyday group talk which combines conversation and argument. Their purpose appears to be as a forum for people to register opinions and to vent feelings. There is a lot of talk but it gets nowhere, for while everyone has a say, no-one appears to listen. There may be little point to listening other than to find provocation for one's own view, pro or con. Pro or con, though, everyone's opinion is presumed to be right (or wrong), for there are no standards and methods by which to assess the several views; there is just agreement and disagreement as an incidental to the expression of views. Hence the topic is not developed, although expansively commented upon; nor are the minds, hearts or behaviours of the participants, although intensively involved. The talk ends when everyone has had their say, perhaps thrice over, or when people are exhausted or frustrated by the endless and fruitless display of felt opinion and impulsive reaction.

These are the preferred ways of talking together in common society, and they are heard often enough in classrooms as well. They make their way effortlessly into classrooms but once inside they remain everyday forms of talk. They differ from discussion in nearly every respect, as just reviewed: topic, turn-taking, purpose, start/finish, structure, process, outcome. Just as different but far more common in classrooms is that style of group talk peculiar to classrooms, called recitation.

Classroom recitation

How can we tell a discussion from a recitation? Three good ways to tell are by the characteristics of the talk, the perceptions of the participants, and the concepts of discussion (this section is from Dillon 1988c). To illustrate all the contrasts, we will use the same two examples – an actual classroom recitation and an actual discussion. A short transcript from each class is reproduced at the end of this book (see transcripts 1 and 2).

These two classrooms will help us to sharpen our notions of what a discussion is and how it differs from a recitation. They are good examples because the two classes are similar except for the fact that one is a recitation and one is a discussion. For instance, both of them are history classes taught in the very same week in the junior year of secondary school (ages 16–17). Both of them are taught by good teachers, yet they make enough mistakes to give us a realistic idea of how things can go in practice. And the students in both classes have the same verbal ability, as measured by the verbal portion of the Preliminary Scholastic Aptitude Test (PSAT). So the differences that we will see between this discussion class and this recitation class are not due to the skill of the teacher, the ability of the students, the level of the school, the time of year, or the nature of the subject matter. Nor is one class a good example of discussion and the other a bad example of recitation. They are both good classes of their type. The difference is due to the processes that teacher and students are engaging in over this subject matter.

What is that difference, and how can we tell? Let us picture ourselves in the corridor of a school. On our left is Mr H's American History class, talking back and forth about the Revolutionary War. On our right is Mr T's European History class, talking back and forth about France under Louis XIV (see transcripts 1 and 2 for a snippet of their talk). Both of them are obviously good classes, interesting lessons taught by skilful teachers to eager students. But the two classes also seem plainly different. In fact, Mr T's class is a discussion, Mr H's a recitation. We can tell the difference by the characteristics of the talk, the perceptions of the participants, and the concepts of discussion.

Characteristics of talk

Recitation is characterized by one way of talking back and forth, discussion by another. The two processes differ on seven noticeable points (there are other points that are not so noticeable). We can actually hear and see a difference in the predominant speaker in Mr H's class and Mr T's class, in the type of exchange, the sequence of speakers, the overall pace, and the kind of questions asked, answers given and evaluations supplied. Table 1.1 conveniently summarizes these differences.

1 Predominant speaker
In recitation there is a predominant speaker, and that is the teacher; typically, the teacher speaks about two-thirds or more of the time. In discussion there might perhaps be a predominant speaker but it will not be the teacher; students will speak half or more of the time. For example, let us look at our illustrative transcripts. In the recitation class, Mr H speaks for 69 per cent of the time; in Mr T's discussion class, the students account for 78 per cent of the talk (the teacher for 22 per cent).

2 Typical exchange
In recitation we hear a characteristic exchange of talk, most easily described as question–answer. And the question–answer is from teacher and student (not from student and teacher). It is actually a three-part exchange: question–answer–evaluation plus next question. And the parts are nearly always played out by teacher–student–teacher. By contrast, that exchange does *not* characterize discussion. Rather, we will hear a mix of statements and questions by a mix of teacher and students.

Table 1.1 Noticeable characteristics of talk in recitation and discussion

Characteristics	Recitation	Discussion
1 Predominant speaker	Teacher two-thirds or more	Students half or more
2 Typical exchange	**Question–answer** 1 Teacher question 2 Student answer 3 Teacher evaluation (plus next question)	**Not question–answer** A mix of statements and questions by a mix of teacher and students
3 Predictable sequence	Teacher–student	A mix of teacher–student, student–teacher, student–student
4 Overall pace	Many, brief, fast exchanges (could be slower)	Fewer, longer, slower exchanges (could not be faster)
5 The question	Not the question itself as asked, but students showing knowledge of answer	The question itself as asked, and the students gaining or using knowledge about the matter in question
6 The answer	1 Predetermined right/wrong 2 Same right answer for all students	1 Indeterminate, determinable, determined and not (but not predetermined) 2 Could be different answers for different students
7 The evaluation	1 'Right/wrong' 2 By teacher only	1 'Agree/disagree' 2 By student and by teacher, also by student of teacher

The difference here is a negative one, not opposites. There seems to be no characteristic exchange in discussion. We might hear some question–answers but they will not *characterize* the exchange. And, since the exchange is a mix of moves by a mix of speakers, we might hear a question from a student as well as from the teacher, and an answer by the teacher as well as by a student. Question–answer characterizes recitation; it does not characterize discussion.

For example, questions account for 78 per cent of Mr H's talk in the recitation class, but for only 11 per cent of Mr T's talk in the discussion. Not at all incidentally, the use of questions helps account for the difference in predominant speaker. A recitation involves more teacher talk, for the fact that the teacher actually speaks twice in each exchange (question, then evaluation plus question). All that the students speak is the answer. And answers are typically short. That also helps to explain two other differences – the predictable sequence and the quicker pace that are typical of recitation but not discussion.

3 Predictable sequence

Recitation has a predictable sequence of talk: first the teacher, then a student will speak. The sequence is almost always teacher–student, nothing else. You can bet your money on that and win nine times out of ten. But if you bet your money on the sequence of talk in discussion, you may well lose half of the time. Discussion has no characteristic sequence of talk. The sequence is a mix of teacher–student, student–teacher and student–student.

For example, 88 per cent of the sequences in Mr H's recitation are teacher–student. In Mr T's discussion, 94 per cent are student–student. The important distinction is not that the discussion is student–student, but that it is *not* wholly teacher–student. It so happens that Mr T's discussion is overwhelmingly student–student, but student–student is not the thing that characterizes discussion. Another discussion class might well have 33 per cent student–student, 33 per cent student–teacher and 33 per cent teacher–student; or 50 per cent teacher–student. What it will *not* have, as a *distinguishing* characteristic, is something approaching Mr H's 88 per cent teacher–student. It is easy to understand why. It follows naturally from the negative fact that question–answer does not characterize discussion. That fact also helps us to understand the difference in overall pace.

4 Overall pace

In a recitation we typically hear many, brief and fast exchanges. In a discussion we will hear fewer, longer and slower exchanges. The pace in a recitation *could* be slower but the pace in discussion could *not* be much faster. For example, the pace in Mr H's recitation involves over six exchanges per minute, with student talk lasting four seconds at a time, on average. By contrast, the pace in Mr T's discussion hardly involves even one exchange per minute, and the students speak for twenty-five seconds at a time.

A striking way to illustrate the contrast is to picture ourselves standing in the middle of that corridor again, with Mr H's recitation class on our left-hand side and Mr T's discussion on our right-hand side. Consider just the exchanges that are reproduced in the transcripts here. Use a stopwatch. Go! By the time that Mr T's class is just completing one single exchange, the *whole* of Mr H's recitation episode will already have flashed by on our left, winning by a mile.

This tortoise-and-hare contrast between these two particular classes of Mr H and Mr T is extreme but it is still perfectly characteristic on both sides. Mr H does indeed ask a lot of questions at a fast pace, overall five to six per minute. He doubles that in some episodes – twelve question–answers in a single minute. He happens to keep up an energetic pace. But even if he 'slowed' down by half, to two to three questions a minute, his class would still be a recitation – only a slower one this time. A recitation could be slower than the frenetic pace in Mr H's class but it would still be characterized, by contrast to a discussion, by many, brief, fast exchanges. That follows naturally from the overriding fact that when he speaks, the teacher is asking questions.

5 The question

The character of the question (or questions) in recitation is quite distinct from that in discussion. For the recitation question, that which is *in* question is not actually the question itself as asked. Something *else* is in question, such as the student's showing knowledge of the answer and the teacher's gaining knowledge that the student knows this answer in this or that way. In discussion the thing that is in question is actually the question that is being asked. And that involves the student's not demonstrating but gaining or using knowledge about the matter in question.

We can't tell this difference by looking at the question. But we can *feel* it when the question is asked aloud. And we can actually *see* proof of it when we hear what follows the answer. For example, Mr H's recitation starts with the main question (not shown in the transcript): 'Why do you think they won, these 13 colonies?' This looks like a question about the reasons that the American colonists won the Revolutionary War; and it looks like students are being asked to think and to reason through the issue, even perhaps to speculate and give their opinions and interpretations. But of course no-one in the room believes any of that for a minute. At least, no-one acts as if they believe it.

The question in Mr T's discussion looks very much the same. The hour begins with Louis XIV's handling of various classes of French society – nobles, peasants, bourgeoisie. Our episode starts with: 'Do you feel that Louis was justified in his treatment of the Huguenots?' That looks like students are being asked to think things through and come up with opinions and reasons, grounds for and against justification. And that's just what everyone in the room starts doing.

In the recitation episode, however, no-one in the room ever acts like that. This is despite the questions that continue to come. The original question soon changes into: 'I want to go into another question about Washington's military capabilities. What was it that made him militarily successful?' And, at the start of our transcript: 'Why else did they win?' So, in both classes we see open, complex, 'higher-cognitive' questions. But they only look alike, they are not alike. They have distinctly different characteristics that neatly serve to distinguish recitation from discussion. We see and hear proof of that when it comes to the answers that are given and then the reactions to the answers.

6 *The answer*
The difference between recitation and discussion is not, as people

often say, that there is a right answer to the recitation question(s). For there are right answers to any question. We realize that for any given question there is an answer (or answers) that is right, the others being wrong. The problem is that we don't always know the right answer, or we disagree over which answer is the right one. It is that point which distinguishes discussion from recitation.

The answer in recitation is *predetermined* to be right or wrong. (Note that the predetermined right answer might actually be a wrong or incorrect answer; an answer is being upheld as the right one.) The question in discussion is *not* predetermined. It is indeterminate, or able to be determined, or sometimes determined and sometimes not. Therefore, in recitation there is one and the same predetermined right answer for all students; in discussion there *could* be a different right answer for each student, depending on the issue, or two right answers for groups of students, or even one right answer that all students come up with – but not a predetermined right answer.

For example, take the question in our recitation episode: 'Why did the colonies win?' We can easily imagine a conference of historians, British and American, or of political scientists, or of military strategists, addressing that question. In fact, that is just the kind of thing that these people do. (Then they write books, one or another of which is adopted for one or another curriculum.) We can imagine their coming to divergent answers to the question – distinct, perhaps even opposing, reasons for victory and success. And we can even imagine them all to conclude to one and the same set of reasons, moreover the very set of reasons that we hear spoken and affirmed in the recitation class. But whereas the historians *discuss* the question, the students do not; whereas the historians may diverge on the answers, the students may not; and whereas the historians might possibly come to one and the same answer, the students must give the one answer. Therefore, contrary to what many people say, the difference between recitation and discussion is not that the recitation is based on fact and the discussion on non-factual matters. Not so. We can hear discussions over factual matters and recitations over matters of opinion.

Now it may well be that there is a difference in the thinking processes going on while *reciting* or *discussing* the answer – regardless of whether the question is factual or interpretive. For example, 29 per cent of student talk in Mr H's recitation is of a 'higher-cognitive' type or level, compared to 87 per cent in Mr T's discussion. (Higher here refers to 'explaining, opining, justifying' *vs* the lower 'defining, interpreting, fact-stating'.) But I myself have seen lessons where students discuss *facts*, and lessons where students *recite* opinions.

Indeed, one of the very best classroom discussions I have ever observed, one every bit as good as Mr T's, was over the question of sexual experience in the student's family life: 'What were the patterns in your family regarding nudity, affection, and talk about sex?' This is obviously a factual question. And, speaking things like this question, the teacher's talk was clearly lower-cognitive. Yet fully half the students' talk was at *higher*-cognitive levels. This was a discussion regarding factual matters, what Roby (1988) calls an 'informational' discussion. (This discussion class appears in transcript 3 and is analysed in Chapter 5.)

It makes no difference whether the question is higher- or lower-cognitive, whether it is simple or complex, whether it is fact or interpretation. What makes the difference is whether the answer to the question is predetermined to be right, whether it is to be recited or discussed. We see proof of that difference not only in the answers that are given but also in what follows upon the answer. Here the proof is as clear as day, and the difference as between day and night.

7 *The evaluation*

After a student speaks in recitation, we always hear 'right/wrong' in so many words, and always from the teacher. In discussion we hear 'agree/disagree' and we hear it from a student or from the teacher. Also in discussion we can hear 'agree/disagree' from a student about what the teacher speaks. In a recitation we never hear 'agree/disagree'; we never hear it from a student, and never about the teacher; nor do we hear 'right/wrong' from a student, whether about another student or the teacher. (No-one has actually to say these very *words*. There are many various ways to give that evaluation, such as 'OK' or 'Well, . . .')

For example, in Mr T's discussion episode we hear a series of students giving different answers to the question: Louis XIV wasn't justified in going as far as he did; he was partially right but; he had no justification; he could justify it to himself. Later we hear a series of 'agree/disagree' both from the students and the teacher. Mr T never says 'right/wrong'. He says: 'OK, I can see where you're coming from, but I don't know if I can totally agree with that'. Sean says that Marty was wrong (not in the sense of 'incorrect' as in 'right/wrong answer'); Marty says that Sean brought up a good point; Diane disagrees ('Well, I don't know . . .'); and Mark says Diane has a good point. We hear none of that in a recitation. All we hear is 'right/wrong', always from the teacher. That is because the answer is predetermined to be right/wrong; and the determination has been made by the teacher (text, curriculum, etc.).

Other differences in the talk characterizing discussion and recitation will be described later in this book (Chapter 5). There, Mr H's recitation class will again be analysed by contrast to discussion – but for a different purpose – using three other discussion classes (transcripts 3, 4 and 5 at the end of this book). For instance, the discussions will be shown to have longer student responses and greater student initiative when the teacher uses non-questioning techniques appropriately.

There are still other differences in talk, and there are differences *other* than in talk. We can tell a discussion from a recitation by the noticeable characteristics of talk – the predominant speaker and exchange, the sequence and pace, the question, answer and evaluation (see Table 1.1 for a summary). This is a useful way to tell the difference, because we can easily see and hear these characteristics. Yet these are not the *essential* differences; they do not actually make a discussion, or a recitation. Other things make for the essential difference. But these essential things are not easily seen and heard. Luckily for us, though, when they are present we can see and hear a distinct difference in the talk.

These other, more important factors include the perceptions of the participants and the concepts of discussion. How do they make the difference, and how can we find out the difference that they make?

Perceptions of participants

The perceptions of people involved in a class can help us to tell whether the class is a discussion. How do *they* see it? We cannot hear or see their perceptions. But we can find them out. For instance, we can ask the teacher and students what they see in this class.

1 Teacher

We might want to ask the teacher any number of things. The one thing we must be sure to find out are his or her purposes. First, has the teacher planned this class session to be a discussion? Second, while teaching it, is the teacher intending to conduct a discussion? If not, we are for all intents and purposes not in a discussion class.

For example, I interviewed Mr H and Mr T a week before observing their classroom teaching. I asked them to tell me a day on which they planned to hold a discussion in class; and that is how we scheduled the day for my visit. I also talked to them just before the lesson in question. It was then that Mr H told me of a change in plan. Because of a switch in the school schedule, his students had only now completed their study projects for the unit on the American Revolution. Tomorrow he planned a discussion. As for today's class, 'I'm afraid it'll be more question–answer than discussion', he said. And so it was.

We should by rights also interview the teacher after the lesson, checking to see what his or her intents were during the actual process that just transpired. I didn't know enough to take that obvious step. But I did check with the students afterwards.

2 Students

The teacher might well be intending a discussion, and yet the students might not perceive the class to be such. If so, when students participate they are not to their intents and purposes participating in a discussion class. We can find out how they see the lesson by asking them, say in an interview or questionnaire. For example, at the end of the lesson, I gave the students in Mr H's class and Mr T's class a questionnaire to fill out. It was made up of two kinds of items. Half the items related to 'teacher empathy' and half to 'group expressiveness' (these were taken from the Teacher–Pupil Relationship Inventory of Barrett-Lennard (1962) and the Group Environment Scale of Moos and Humphrey (1974)).

Empathy describes how the students perceive the teacher as welcoming and wanting to understand what the students think and say in class. Here are one positive and one negative item:

> This teacher wants to understand how I see things.
> This teacher looks at what I say from his own point of view.

The higher the score, the greater the perceived empathy. On a scale of 10, students rated Mr H's recitation class 4.8, as against 7.1 for Mr T's discussion. So, the students saw the discussion as more a matter of having what they say understood.

Expressiveness. How do students see the students' expressiveness in this class? Positive and negative items include:

> In this class you find out what other people really think about things. // When students in here disagree, they usually say so.

> It's hard to tell how people in this class are feeling. // People are careful about what they say in this class.

On a scale of 10, the students rated Mr H's recitation only 2.2 in expressiveness, as against 6.5 for Mr T's discussion. So, the students saw the discussion but not the recitation as a place where students were actually expressing their thoughts.

These contrasting perceptions also show up in the different ways that students participated in the two classes. For example, 41 per cent of Mr H's students but 77 per cent of Mr T's spoke up in class, Mr H's for 4 seconds at a time and Mr T's for 25 seconds.

Of course, there are many perceptions that we might wish to know from the participants, and various other techniques for finding these out. The main point is that the perceptions of the participants are one of the ways to tell whether a class is a discussion. We can see only certain things and however we might see the class, we need to know how *they* see it.

Concepts of discussion

The most important way to tell a discussion is by the concepts of discussion. These are the things that make the class a discussion, and they show the essential difference between discussion and recitation. Unfortunately, we cannot see or hear these things in the classroom. They are the most important but the least noticeable features of discussion.

These concepts are quite abstract – ideas, notions, definitions and the like. They are not like the characteristics of talk, which we can easily see and hear. They are not like the perceptions of participants, which we can fairly easily find out by asking. Rather, we have to infer and analyse these concepts, and try to discover how they apply to the classroom we are in. Let us see how we might do that, by comparing what we know of our two classes – those of Mr H and Mr T – against abstract models and principles of discussion.

1 Models

Some useful models of discussion have been worked out by Roby (1988). On the basis of many complicated factors, he distinguishes three types of discussion: informational, problematical and dialectical. At each end of this continuum is a type of pseudo-discussion – bull session and quiz show.

A *quiz show* is not a discussion. It can be briefly described as a conversation that is text- or teacher-centred. There are a lot of teacher questions; the teacher has the answers and the students are to get them and get them right. With this abstract model in our mind we can walk into Mr H's class and surely tell that it is a quiz show. In a *dialectical discussion*, students and teacher resolve opposing opinions through inquiry and synthesis of the truth elements in each. They question the opinions being proffered by others and then they question the opinion that they themselves are proffering. This abstract model lets us tell that Mr T's class is a discussion, a dialectical one.

2 Principles

Many principles of discussion have been identified by Bridges (1979). He specifies all the necessary conditions for us to say that people are engaged in a discussion of something. The result is a comprehensive set of logical conditions, moral dispositions, intellectual qualities and dimensions of openness – all of which were described earlier in this chapter. How might these principles help us to tell that T but not H is a discussion?

Here is a good chance for you, the reader, to do a practical exercise. The principles of discussion are set out in Table 1.2 as a checklist for rating the two different classes. Since we can hardly see most of these things in front of our face, we have to infer their presence in the class. By now you know quite a bit about H and T, so you should be in a fairly good position to rate them on at least some of these points. Then you will see the essential difference between discussion and recitation, and you will know for sure why Mr T's class is really a discussion.

Two other classrooms are listed in Table 1.2 for you to rate: some other classroom that you might wish to visit to observe the discussion, and your own classroom. You can get down to the realistic task of trying to find these points in live classes in your own school. And you might also try two further exercises in these classes, by asking for the perceptions of the participants and by listening for the characteristics of the talk; use Table 1.1 as a checklist. These are three good ways to tell a discussion.

Usage of discussion

A final point of contrast is the actual use of discussion in practice. We should know that discussion is not a common form of discourse in society, much less in school. The other, even contrary forms of group talk are much preferred socially and much more practised scholastically. For instance, recitation is the predominant form of interactive talk in classrooms.

Discussion is hardly ever heard in classrooms. Teachers may well say that they use discussion a lot, but their self-reports are demonstrably unreliable. And that is not because teachers are confused about the terms they use or don't really know what discussion is. Thus, whereas a high-school English teacher reported discussion to be her preferred method of teaching, used at least three or four times a week – with recitation specifically her next preference – observation revealed that she used discussion 5

Table 1.2 Criteria for analysing discussion classes

Criteria[a]	Transcripts		Classrooms	
	1. H Recitation	2. T Discussion	Observed class	Your own class
Logical conditions				
1 Talk to one another	————	————	————	————
2 Put forward various views on the subject	————	————	————	————
3 Listen to one another	————	————	————	————
4 Respond to one another	————	————	————	————
5 Intend to develop understanding of the topic	————	————	————	————
Moral dispositions				
1 Reasonableness	————	————	————	————
2 Peaceableness and orderliness	————	————	————	————
3 Truthfulness	————	————	————	————
4 Freedom	————	————	————	————
5 Equality	————	————	————	————
6 Respect for persons	————	————	————	————

Intellectual qualities

1 Respect for opinions of others _____
2 Scepticism of authority _____
3 Diversity _____
4 Responsiveness _____
5 Judiciousness _____
6 Reflectiveness _____
7 Evidence _____
8 Clarity _____
9 Conciseness _____
10 Consistency _____

Openness dimensions

1 Subject open for discussion _____
2 Open-minded participants _____
3 Open to all contributions _____
4 Open to all persons _____
5 Open time-limit _____
6 Open outcomes _____
7 Overt purposes and practices _____
8 Open-ended conclusion _____

[a]From Bridges (1979, 1988, 1990).

per cent of the time and recitation 45 per cent (Conner and Chalmers-Neubauer 1989). Although two dozen middle school teachers of various subjects reported using discussion – moreover defining it by contrast to related forms of talk – only seven could be observed using discussion; the others used recitation and lecture with question–answer (Alvermann *et al.* 1990).

Extensive observations of one thousand elementary and secondary classrooms across the United States have revealed that discussion – undifferentiated back-and-forth talk – could probably be seen only 4–7 per cent of the time (Goodlad 1984). Intensive observations of three dozen fifth-grade maths and social science classrooms in a US city have revealed discussion – by specific contrast to recitation, also observed – being used in no more than 3 per cent of the instructional episodes (Stodolsky *et al.* 1981).

No-one can be sure of just how widely discussion is being used, but as far as we can tell it is minimal, scant, almost non-existent. Discussion is an ancient and essential educative activity that is rarely practised in our schools.

Suppose that we aspire to engage in discussion in our own circumstances. What do we need? The next chapters address our needs point for point. We will need a subject matter to discuss (Chapter 2), a class willing to discuss it (Chapter 3), some conduct (Chapter 4) and language (Chapter 5) appropriate to discussion, and finally an overwhelming rationale for discussion (Chapter 6). That may sound like a lot for us to acquire, but these matters are basic, even rather simple. For instance, while we do need a subject matter for discussion, we also need a subject matter for any mode of talk when we are teaching; we have to talk about *something*. Moreover, none of these matters is fancy and sophisticated; all of them are within the reach of the willing teacher. If we are willing, we too can join in discussion.

2

WHAT THINGS ARE DISCUSSED?

When we ask about the subject of discussion, we want to know about the things that people discuss. People discuss some topic, and that topic is an aspect of some subject matter. What constitutes a topic for discussion? What subject matters can be discussed? Topic and subject matter are given form in a question for discussion. What is the question that people discuss?

In general, the thing that people discuss is a topic that is in question for them. And in principle, any subject matter can be discussed. It can be discussed at any level of the topic, from elementary through to the rarified, and at any level of schooling, from primary to university.

In practice, however, discussion is reserved for the more erudite graduates at advanced levels of education, in selected classes or elective seminars on recondite aspects of one or two subject matters in the arts and some humanities, perhaps. This practice is travesty. It betrays both the truth and our young. The truth is that children and youngsters, pupils and students, and scholars of any age can discuss any subject matter in any of its respects. Topics for discussion abound in the subject matters taught in kindergarten and in the first and second years of school. These are the things that children wonder about the subject matter. The thing that is in question for them becomes the topic for discussion.

TOPIC OF DISCUSSION

What makes something into a topic for discussion? A matter can be discussed if there is some question about it. 'Something in question' is a topic for discussion. 'Something in question' refers not so much to a matter considered in itself as to *our relation* with that matter. That is, a matter comes to be in question when we experience a question in relation to it. The matter is settled – it is no longer something in question – when we have resolved our question about it. The things that people discuss are things that they have some question about. Hence, one and the same matter may well figure as a topic of discussion for some people, because they experience a question about it, while remaining an object of quiet satisfaction or even unthinking neglect for other people, because the matter in not in question for them.

What is it about the something-in-question that people can have questions about? In principle, we can have a question about any aspect of any matter. A topic for discussion can be anything that perplexes us, that we wonder about, that we are unsure of, that we need to work out. In general, there is something about the matter that we want to understand, to evaluate or to resolve.

Thus, the 'what' that is discussed depends on the 'who' that is discussing and the 'why' that they have for discussing it. In education, students discuss all manner of aspects about a subject matter, according as they experience questions about these various aspects. Even if teacher, text and test exhibit certainty about a matter, students will still need to discuss it if they are uncertain about it. Moreover, educators rightly desire that students engage in proper processes as they come to learn a subject matter. A textbook may display a proposition about the subject matter and a teacher may lecture on it, without the students coming to understand it; in that case, discussion may be the process through which students appropriately learn this aspect of the subject matter. Still further, educators also aspire to help students to learn how to learn, along with learning given aspects of the subject matter. In that respect, discussion may serve purposes of increasing the students' powers of understanding subject matters, as well as increasing the number of things that they understand about this subject matter.

Even in the extreme case where the teacher and other adults already understand full well everything that there is to know about the subject matter, still this matter can become a fit topic for class discussion – if it is *something in question for students*. Students may wonder what to think and how to act about this matter. They seek to know or understand something about it, to appreciate and judge it in some respect, to resolve and decide it. They need to form ideas, sentiments, values and actions concerning it. They further need to learn how to go about knowing and understanding, judging and resolving matters. And they need to accomplish these learnings through an activity or process that is in line with the educational purpose as well as conducive to proper learning of the subject matter. On any of these grounds, a matter can be fit as a topic for class discussion. But in which classes, which subject matters?

SUBJECT MATTERS

In which subject matters can a class hold a discussion? In principle, students can discuss in all subject matters in all classes. The basic requirement is that there is something in question about the subject matter. That something-in-question becomes the topic for discussion, whatever the subject matter that is being taught and learned in that class.

Yet some subject matters are regarded as more suitable for discussion than others, while certain ones are regarded as not discussable at all. The requirement of a topic in question is widely mistaken to exempt from discussion 'hard' subject matters like mathematics and science, together with facts in all subjects, including 'soft' ones like literature and social studies. This view, though widely shared by educators and uneducated people, is none the less uninformed and anti-educative.

There are controversial issues in the hard as in the soft subjects, and issues other than controversial ones in all subjects. Moreover, any matter at all can come to issue, including a matter of fact. The question of facticity may well arise; and where the facts are not dubitable but agreed, there remain other grounds for discussing even hard facts, while even in hard sciences there remain things other than facts to discuss.

Furthermore, education requires the discussion of all subject matters in any of their respects. But why discuss a fact or other known matters? Well, we may question whether or wherein it is a fact. Where there is no question of that, we may question how it came to be a fact. If that is not in question, we may further question what meaning, significance or worth it may have, how we are to use it or what we are to do with it. Students may discuss all of these things about facts and about other matters too – theories and concepts, opinions and hypotheses, principles, methods and conclusions. They discuss to learn these aspects of the subject matter; further, to learn the processes surrounding these aspects; and still further, to learn to think, talk and act about this subject matter; and, finally, to learn how to learn this and other subject matters.

Let us now examine how these general considerations apply to the particular subject matters of mathematics and sciences. We will not proceed to other subject matters, because our task is not to detail how each and every subject matter in school can be discussed. Far from it, we have advanced a general principle and relevant considerations to propose that all subject matters can be discussed. What is called for now is not to show how that principle applies in every case but only in those test cases where others hold that it does not apply. Few people doubt that the proposed considerations apply to familiar areas such as literature, philosophy and social studies. Here we will show how they apply *equally* and *in the same way* to the supposedly undiscussable subjects of maths and science.

To show this point we will recur to specialists in these subject fields, merely reviewing the considerations that they identify for discussion in their area. These will be seen as particular applications of the general principles and considerations that we have advanced for discussion in all subject areas.

Readers who would like to pursue these matters can look in journals and magazines for teachers of these subjects, those with titles like 'X Education' and 'Y Teachers' (e.g. *Social Studies*

Education). To find these scattered sources, try using an index or catalogue for 'discussion', or ask a librarian for help in finding articles on discussion in a particular field.

Mathematics

'What is the point of group discussion in mathematics?' is the title of one article (Hoyles 1985). The point is to understand and to integrate maths concepts, on the view that 'mathematical ideas are susceptible to a variety of interpretations' (ibid.: p. 207). Through discussion the students come to:

- articulate and understand their own ideas for themselves;
- to elaborate their ideas and communicate them to others;
- to clarify and modify their ideas from the cognitive conflict and dynamic feedback of social interaction.

This use of discussion rests on the definition of mathematical understanding as the ability to form a view of the mathematical idea, to reflect upon it and to use it appropriately, to communicate it effectively, to reflect on someone else's perspective of the idea, and to incorporate another's perspective or to challenge and logically reject that alternative view. That view of mathematical understanding may itself open a discussion: What is mathematical understanding?

Physics

A group of physicists in England, mainly teachers in higher education, gathered at a conference and worked out this set of aims for group discussion in physics. Despite their claim that science teaching is vastly different from arts teaching, these points 'seem remarkably like what one would expect a group of literature and philosophy teachers to produce in similar circumstances' (Rudduck 1978: 6). Indeed, we could remove the word 'physics' from these statements and use them to describe almost any subject matter. Showing these points to specialists in another field would be an interesting exercise.

1 To help students communicate as physicists, knowing the language, standards and structure of knowledge in physics.

2 To provide practice in the application of principles.
3 To encourage the development of critical standards and a questioning attitude towards evidence.
4 To extend the range of ideas available to an individual.
5 To help students appreciate that physics is about people.
6 To provide an opportunity for students to clarify their thinking through talking, using the group as a critical sounding board.
7 To build opportunities for the critical examination of individual or group assignments.
8 To encourage familiarity with significant achievements or achievers in physics.

These physicists appeared to have had in mind the concern to disabuse students of the notion that physics is essentially about facts and to encourage them to see the provisional character of knowledge in physics and to respond to the controversies that are central to the discipline (Rudduck 1978: 7).

Biology

In agricultural boarding schools for secondary students in Israel, students used group discussion to deliberate over ways of controlling a biological process that would enhance their farming activities (Dreyfus and Lieberman 1981). For instance, to preserve the microbiological quality of milk from their cows, the students had to consider the nature and ecology of identified microorganisms, their biochemical influence on milk, and the methods for measuring their activity. Observation of their discussions revealed several grounds and reasons for their discussion activity (ibid.: pp. 154, 156).

1 It is difficult to identify the scientific principles relevant to a concrete problem.
2 It is difficult to discover the best method of application of these principles to this context.
3 Different approaches to solution may be equally legitimate theoretically and attractive practically.
4 Subjects related to the acquisition and application of the needed knowledge had to be discussed.

5 Discussion helps students to discover meanings, implications and uses of a biological concept.

Chemistry

An introductory chemistry course at an American university was dramatically changed by emphasizing discussion instead of lecture (Fasching and Erickson 1985), on the grounds that discussion would make the course more consistent with its claims to stress three broad processes:

1 *Scientific method*: the 'puzzling process' of investigation.
2 *Problem solving*: analysing problems, hypothesizing, experimentation.
3 *Reasoning*: explaining, predicting, concluding.

Half of the meeting time was devoted to group discussion, and one-third of laboratory sessions were devoted to small group research projects. Before this use of discussion, students could only memorize and recall information and use specific information to solve explicit problems with given relationships and stated rules or formulae to use. Afterwards, the examinations could ask students to analyse data, solve complex problems and design experimental procedures (ibid.: p. 845).

Genetics

A college-level genetics course used discussion for issues concerning the application of new genetic knowledge and technologies, such as alphafetoprotein screening for neural tube defects (Hendrix *et al*. 1983). The discussions were used to identify and clarify the following:

• pertinent data from various disciplines;
• relevant values held by the student and his or her peers;
• alternative solutions to the issue;
• those solutions seen as morally and ethically acceptable by society.

The curriculum

Discussion is used throughout the entire curriculum at St. John's College in Annapolis, Maryland and Santa Fe, New Mexico (see St John's College 1993). All students discuss all subject matters in all classes throughout all four years.

What do these students discuss? In pursuit of liberal education, they discuss the great books of the Western heritage. They learn not by lecture and recitation but by discussion, and they discuss not textbooks but original writings by the most pre-eminent thinkers. They read and discuss the great books in literature, philosophy and theology, in history and social science, and in mathematics and natural sciences.

Again restricting ourselves to mathematics and science, we note that first-year students read and discuss, among many other works, Lavoisier's *Elements of Chemistry* and Harvey's *Motion of the Heart and Blood*, while second-year students discuss *On the Revolution of the Spheres* by Copernicus, plus Descartes' *Geometry* and Pascal's *Generation of Conic Sections*. In the third year, students read and discuss Newton's *Principia Mathematica* and Galileo's *Two New Sciences*, along with Huygen's *Treatise on Light* and Dedekind's *Essay on the Theory of Numbers*. In the fourth year, they discuss Millikan's *The Electron*, Darwin's *Origin of the Species*, Mendel's *Experiments in Plant Hybridization* and, of course, selected papers by Einstein. The students read and discuss many other books, such as Faraday's *Experimental Researches on Electricity and Magnetism*, and many other papers by Bernouilli, Heisenberg, Bohr and the like.

Discussion of mathematics helps students to think about 'what it means to count and measure things in the universe', and further, 'what it means to come to know something' (St John's College 1993: 13). Here are some of the questions discussed in their mathematics classes:

1 Why and how do mathematical proofs carry such conviction?
2 What is a mathematical system and what are its proper beginnings and ends?
3 What is the relation of logic to mathematics?
4 Are there 'mathematical objects'?

5 How might the discoverer of a particular theorem have come to see it?

The study of science includes experimental work in the laboratory as well as readings of the original works of scientists. But in this curriculum the laboratory sessions include not just experimental work but a 'full and free discussion of the instruments and the principles involved in it', with the purpose of achieving 'an intimate mixture of critical discussion and empirical inquiry' (ibid.: p. 17).

These examples show us how, what, wherein and why such supposedly undiscussable subject matters as mathematics and science can in fact be discussed. Topics in these and all other subject matters can be discussed when something about them is in question. Something can be in question about them even in the first year of school. What can be discussed? Any aspect of any subject matter at any level of school can in principle be discussed, in any class, by any students.

QUESTION FOR DISCUSSION

Looking at our general question, 'What things are discussed?' under another light, we see that people discuss *a question*. The topic and the subject matter they are concerned about are incorporated into the form of a discussion question. What is the question that people discuss? What makes it a discussion question? On the view that people in discussion form a community of inquiry (see Chapter 3), the discussion question expresses the group predicament and invites joint inquiry.

Expresses group predicament

As the object of discussion, the question expresses the group's predicament. This predicament describes the group's relation to the subject matter being discussed. The question captures part of the plight of the group in its present state, arising from its previous involvement with the subject matter and eventually resolving in other involvements to come. What is in question for us now, given what we have been doing with this subject matter and what we plan to do with it later?

The discussion question formulates an interrogative matter that the group aspires to answer. If the group does not need an answer, there is no question about it; and if the group does not want an answer, there will be no discussion of it. In that failed case, the interrogative is not a question for discussion but a focus for topical commentary, conversation and other non-discussion talk.

A discussion question also formulates a matter that requires a group to answer, and further requires to be answered through discussion. Some questions are better answered by individuals, but most group questions and even most individual questions are better answered by a group. Some group questions are better answered through research and some through other group processes rather than discussion. That will depend on the nature of the group's predicament in relation to the subject matter. By definition, a discussion question is the object of group discussion. Other questions are addressed by other processes, whether group or individual.

What are the kinds of questions that are discussed? In general terms, the group's predicament concerns what to think and how to act about the subject matter:

- *What to think?* includes questions to know and to understand the matter. Knowing and understanding include questions of fact and meaning, interpretation and explanation, and the rest. These are typical questions in school.
- *How to act?* includes questions to resolve and to decide the matter. These in turn include how to apply or to otherwise use the matter, and what to do with it or about it or in face of it. Some of these are policy questions and questions of procedure or next steps to take. Others involve resolutions, solutions, decisions and actions generally.
- *What to think/act?* represents the conjunction of thought and action or the analytical middle ground between pure thought and brute action. This category includes questions to appreciate and to judge the matter. That includes how to evaluate it and what stance to take respecting it. They are questions

involving sentiment and emotion, worth, values, beliefs and attitudes.

A given question for discussion will likely be one of these questions. These are the questions that people discuss – what to think and how to act about the subject matter under discussion.

Invites joint inquiry

The discussion question invites joint inquiry by rallying the powers and purposes of the group in its present predicament regarding the subject matter, and attaching them in address to the question. The question does not discourage inquiry or dissipate joint effort by inviting their contraries, such as debate and argument, confused and wandering conversation, single-answer searches and individual spin-offs. These contraries may ensue from the form and content of questions that are not in fact discussion questions. Such a question may be proposed for discussion but it fails. People do not discuss it, it is not a question for discussion.

A discussion question is an interrogative sentence, not a word or phrase. 'Abortion', 'the economy', 'Vietnam' and the like are neither questions nor topics for discussion, despite being fatuously referred to by politicians and the media as 'the issues'. Public discourse over such matters is so messy partly because everyone is talking about different, unidentified aspects and questions about the matter; no-one can begin to understand the other, but presuming that the other is speaking to the same issue as they are, everyone takes the discourse perversely.

A question formulated as yes/no or either/or invites dispute or choice instead of discussion. Yes/no questions provide a single, pre-identified proposition for the group to accept or reject. Either/or questions provide two pre-identified alternatives for the group to choose between. Both forms of question invite people to take and to defend sides rather than to inquire into the issue and identify and develop possible resolutions of it. A discussion question permits a range of answers and openness to alternatives not yet identified.

A discussion question formulates the *question* about the matter, not an answer or solution, and not some partial or biased view of it. For example, here is a supervisor's solution-laden question about managing a work situation (Maier 1963: 62):

> How can I transfer a man who is popular in the group but disrupts the work of others, without causing resentment?

Here is a confused either/or question that invites choice or taking sides rather than solving a problem:

> If a female employee accuses her supervisor of making unwelcome advances toward her, and if he denies everything, should the company discharge the supervisor, the employee, or both?

Here is a yes/no question that is loaded, proposed by a student for class discussion (Barnlund and Haiman 1960: 69):

> Is it fair for the Women's Christian Temperance Union to further its beliefs and practices in view of the fact that a man's personal habits are his own business and should not be interfered with by society?

Here are questions that are loaded, but not yes/no or either/or (Phillips *et al.* 1979: 153):

- How can the university be prevented from ripping off the students?
- How can we stop the potentially disastrous increase in the number of nuclear power plants?

Here are five different forms of a question for a discussion group. The first is broad and ambiguous, the second is yes/no, and the third either/or. The remaining forms further specify the question that the group might fruitfully discuss.

1 What can we do to meet future energy needs?
2 Should we encourage the development of nuclear energy?
3 Do we want nuclear energy or fossil fuels?
4 What proposals do we want our congressman to support in the field of energy?
5 What advice do we wish to give our congressman regarding our position on nuclear reactors in our region?

A useful exercise for the reader would be to devise variou... formulations for the defective questions illustrated here, in an effort to form a discussion question. Or the reader might work out various versions of a question for discussion in his and her own class circumstance. Detailed help on formulating questions in various ways, and on the different answers that can be given to various forms of questions, can be found in *The Practice of Questioning* (Dillon 1990). Here our task is not to describe question formulation or to advise on how to formulate a discussion question. Rather, it is to show that a discussion question invites joint inquiry, whereas other questions discourage it and instead invite the contrary of discussion.

When people meet to discuss things, they form a community of inquiry in address to the question for discussion. A discussion question expresses the group's predicament in relation to the subject matter, and by its form and content it invites joint inquiry. In general, the questions that people discuss concern what to think and how to act about the subject matter under discussion. Those are the things that are discussed. Who, now, are the people that discuss these things? (Chapter 3).

WHO ENGAGES IN DISCUSSION?

When we ask about the people who discuss things, we want to know about the participants, the leader and the group. What are they like? What characteristics must students, teacher and class have in order to engage in discussion? In general, the people who engage in discussion are those who have a question about the topic and who want to talk it over in the group.

PARTICIPANTS/STUDENTS

What do students need in order to participate in discussion? Along with having a question about the topic, they must have a disposition to discuss it. A range of skills is also involved but not as prerequisites. Almost any child can join in discussion.

Question

To discuss a topic, people need to have some question about it. They wonder about it in some respect, they are perplexed, uncertain, intrigued, curious, not quite sure about it. It is an issue for them, something they need to resolve. It is a problem, something they need to solve. It is a question, something they need to answer.

In general, the questions we discuss are what to think and how to act about the subject matter under discussion. There is something about it that we feel we need to know or to understand, to appreciate or to judge, to resolve or to decide. If we experience nothing of the sort about the subject matter, then we cannot discuss it. For, we would have no willingness to discuss it; it would be pointless to discuss.

People do not discuss topics that they feel they know everything about or understand perfectly well, thank you. Or they already know or understand enough, all that they need to know about it. The question does not arise for them. People do not discuss matters whose meaning, significance and worth are plain to them, nor sentiments and values that are incontestable. It would be out of the question for them to discuss such things. People do not discuss decisions and actions they are resolved to take. Their mind is made up, the subject matter is closed, it is not an issue for them.

If we do experience some question over the subject matter, we are in a position to discuss it. But we must further be disposed to discuss it. (We commonly do many other things with an issue than discuss it.)

Disposition

The disposition to discuss is a *basic willingness to talk things over with other people*. We want to explore the matter with them, hear other views, and come up with a good answer to our question, one that satisfies us in some respect.

That basic willingness embraces as a matter of course a series of other sentiments or attitudes such as open-mindedness, reasonableness, responsiveness, respect for other opinions, and the like – those, for example, identified by Bridges (1979) and listed in Chapter 1. These form part and parcel of the fundamental disposition to discuss. And like the willingness to discuss, these associated attitudes are basic, not advanced or elevated requirements. We have to share them at least to some minimal extent. We do not have to exhibit them to the highest degree.

People do not need an array of virtues and excellences just in order to join in discussion. They need not have attained the heights and perfections of sentiment just to be able to talk things over with other people. All they need is a basic willingness to discuss.

Without this disposition people cannot discuss. To the extent that they do enjoy this disposition, they may be engaged in discussion. As they willingly engage in discussion, they naturally assume such attitudes as open-mindedness and responsiveness. For, having a question and being disposed to talk it over, they cannot but wish to hear various views and to decide upon one more satisfying than the view that they already have on the question under discussion. So, people who are disposed to discuss will also show these other dispositions to some degree. The requirement is not that they exhibit these to a high degree. Rather, if people have none of these they will not discuss; if they have these at least to some degree, to that extent they will discuss.

Skills

Skills are also involved in discussion but not as prerequisites. That is, people are not required to have an array of skills in order for them to participate in discussion. We can make long lists of the communication skills involved in discussion, the interaction skills, the cognitive and social skills. We can also identify intelligence, experience, knowledge, wisdom and other accomplishments exhibited in discussion. These accomplishments and skills may be required for a high-level discussion. But they are not basic requirements for discussion.

No-one needs intellectual, communication and interaction skills or other accomplishments in order to participate in discussion. The youngest children in our schools can think and wonder, they can talk and listen, they can join and work together. And so, *the youngest children in our schools can discuss.* Their discussion might not be an advanced one. But first-grade discussions are no less discussions than college-level ones are.

Far from being a prerequisite, skills and accomplishments are actually developed through discussion. These are things that educators seek to provide children with. They are part of the reason that children are in school in the first place, and why discussion should be used to educate them. Yet these are also and quite oddly the very things that many educators mistake to be grounds for *not* using discussion with younger children. Hence the school may withhold from children the very educative activity that can provide them with such goods, all the way up to university where graduates still have not learned how to hold a good discussion.

Discussion is a fundamental human activity. It may be practised to refinement by cultivated personages. And it may also be done at a basic yet complete and genuine level by uneducated folk, callow youth, mere novices and primary pupils. As educators, we must not wait until students have achieved maturity and erudition before permitting them to join in discussion of subject matters. To the contrary, we are obligated to impress discussion upon them at the very start of schooling.

Yet our language and concepts for discussion make it appear to be an advanced and elevated activity, above and beyond the reach of younger students. After all, these students are – again by our language and concepts for schooling – still only primary, elementary and intermediate. This is merely to mistake the words for the thing they describe. Because our vocabulary for discussion is abstract, academic and sophisticated, we think the activity of discussion must be like that, too.

To correct this mistaken view, consider this conception of discussion:

> Discussion is a collaborative pursuit consisting of group talk over a common area of inquiry in which the participants are disposed to be open to a variety of points of view, display an attitude of attentiveness and responsiveness while demonstrating a willingness to participate.

Modestly elevated in academic language, this statement in fact was made for discussions that were observed in kindergarten classrooms, with children aged five or so. The author, Richard Bernier (1993), asked: What is the character of discussion in the kindergarten classroom? His observations and analyses of three classrooms revealed these characteristics of discussion in kindergarten:

- a common topic of interest;
- a felt freedom to talk;
- a sense of deeper personal involvement;
- elaboration of ideas;
- alternative explanations and representations of subject matter;
- comments on previous statements;
- responses to other children, not just the adult;
- children initiating the talk;
- an unpredictable turn allocation;
- outcomes which are not predetermined.

These are the very characteristics that have been identified by theorists of discussion and studied by researchers in college and secondary classrooms. And here they are, displayed by five-year-old kindergarten pupils. These children too can discuss, even though our language and concepts for discussion make it seem an impossibly removed activity for little children. Although these observations do not constitute a formal research project, the conclusions that Bernier (1993) draws from them accord with everything that I know about discussion:

> In sum, discussion can be observed in kindergarten classrooms . . . The discussions I observed were not of a high level and the talk over subject matter was mostly exploratory. Nevertheless, kindergarten pupils did discuss.

In order to participate in discussion, kindergarten pupils and any other students have some question about the subject matter and some disposition to discuss it, a basic willingness to talk the matter over with others. Possessed of the question and disposition, students will need only a willing teacher to help them in discussion.

LEADER/TEACHER

What must a teacher have in order to lead a discussion? About all that a teacher needs is a fundamental disposition in favour of discussion, along with some attitudes allied with discussion. The teacher might well also possess many accomplishments of discussion leadership, but these are not requirements for leading a discussion. Most teachers would, however, need development as a discussion leader, making efforts to learn and to practise discussion. The basic requirements, though, are simple.

Fundamental disposition

The one thing that the teacher needs is a disposition in favour of discussion. This disposition comes down to a basic willingness *to have the class discuss*, together with a willingness *to help the class discuss*. No-one could lead a discussion without such a disposition; the process led by such a person would be something other than discussion.

The teacher who is so favourably disposed additionally aspires, in his and her character as a pedagogue, to help the class *to learn how to discuss* at the same time as, and as part of, helping the class to discuss the topic in question. The individual serves both as discussion leader and discussion teacher, leading the actual discussion and teaching about discussion.

That is a hard task, and achieving it is one of the accomplishments of teaching. Yet no teacher is required to be an accomplished discussion leader. All that the willing teacher is being asked to do is to conduct a discussion – to join with students in the basic activity, to do it as well as they can, and to try a bit better next time. The discussion that they hold may be elementary, and it may even be rudimentary, but elementary and rudimentary discussions are no less discussions than the most sophisticated ones are.

The fundamental disposition is a willingness to have the class to discuss and to help the class discuss and to learn to discuss.

Allied attitudes

The teacher who is thus disposed towards discussion holds, almost as a matter of course, democratic sentiments and educational purposes conducive to discussion. The alliance of these terms is nicely expressed in book titles such as *Democracy through Discussion* (Lasker 1949) and *Education, Democracy and Discussion*

(Bridges 1979). As attitudes, these terms describe a posture – the stances that teachers take and the commitments they make as part of their undertaking of discussion in the classroom.

Democratic sentiments incline the teacher to a broadly liberal posture towards society, knowledge and authority – by contrast to a posture that is broadly authoritarian. In *Democracy through Discussion*, Bruno Lasker (1949: 160) concludes that other aptitudes are subsidiary to this main requirement: 'the leader must have faith in democracy'.

No technique or skill can substitute for this attitude. To the contrary, discussion techniques and skills proceed from it. No-one not possessed of these sentiments could lead a discussion. For instance, a teacher with broadly authoritarian sentiments towards knowledge could never hold a discussion that is 'open' in the various dimensions identified by David Bridges (1979) and listed in Chapter 1. Such a teacher would instead lead with skill and technique some non-discussion group process, perhaps recitation.

The *educational purposes* of the teacher must be appropriate for discussion, otherwise the attempt to discuss will be not only misguided but also miseducative. These purposes are prior to the use of discussion, for it is they which properly animate its use. Teachers who use discussion perceive that it promises to serve an educational purpose in their classroom circumstance. Where a teacher does not have the purpose, he or she will also not have the willingness to discuss. It is pointless to hold a discussion when not serviceable to purpose.

Many a teacher who has experienced a failed or frustrated discussion has made the attempt at cross-purposes to begin with. Discussion turns out not to suit their purposes, so the classroom process shifts towards something more suitable, as recitation or lecture. Many educational purposes and pedagogical practices in schools, perhaps the majority, run counter to discussion. And many a hearty effort to change teachers' practices in favour of discussion has been thwarted by running across the teacher's practical purposes (e.g. Alvermann and Hayes 1989, to be described in a subsequent section).

Accomplishments

Nothing further is required to qualify the teacher to lead a discussion. That is, what characteristics are required for a teacher to lead a discussion? The teacher needs the willingness to discuss, together with the democratic sentiments and educational purposes necessary for discussion.

Accomplishments are not required of the teacher. Any number of skills and abilities, virtues and excellences may be involved in accomplished leadership of discussion, but they are not a basic requirement for the teacher who aspires to hold a discussion in class. The teacher may happily gain in these respects as time and experience move along. But the teacher need not and must not await accomplishment before conducting a discussion.

Many other characteristics of a discussion leader can be listed – there are long lists in the literature. But these characteristics turn out to be not further requirements but enumerated details and specifications of the few basic requirements. For example, here is a good list from the tradition of liberal education (Greene 1954). The teacher as discussion leader should possess:

1 A reflective, speculative approach to the subject.
2 A liberal *vs* authoritarian attitude about conflicting opinions.
3 Genuine respect for student minds and interest in student reactions.
4 Be really baffled by the great problems of various kinds in the different spheres of life.
5 Be really persuaded that the search for truth must be a cooperative venture even with the humblest of inquirers.

These five points appear to restate the allied attitude of democratic sentiments, and perhaps represent implications of the fundamental disposition of willingness to discuss.

Endless other matters are also involved in discussion. Evidently, the teacher has to act and to talk while leading a discussion. These matters of how to act and how to talk in discussion are addressed in Chapters 4 and 5. Here we address what the teacher needs to have or to be like in order to lead a discussion. These requirements are few, simple and basic. They require no special sophistication or training, no advanced status or refined gifts.

When we list every possible item that may be involved in leading discussion, and when we highlight the numerous skills and abilities constituting accomplished discussion leadership, we overwhelm the teacher who aspires to practise discussion, incorrectly leaving the impression that the ordinary teacher stands little chance of becoming a discussion leader. The excellences are forbidding, the details discouraging. They make discussion appear to be an advanced method for the experienced and sophisticated teacher, and an activity reserved for the more advanced and learned students. That is not so. Discussion is within the reach of willing teachers and students in everyday classrooms.

Development

Teachers naturally aspire to develop their discussion leadership. How might a teacher learn to lead a discussion?

Individual efforts

Alone, if need be, any teacher can learn about discussion through the following five methods:

1 *Study*: reading good books and articles about discussion, perhaps taking a good course or workshop on it. (Watch out for the bad ones!) Pick a reading or two from the references listed here in this book.
2 *Observation*: seeing discussion in action, by visiting classrooms and methodically noting selected aspects of the discussion process. Watch especially the students. If nothing else, analyse the transcripts of discussion that appear at the end of this book.
3 *Participation*: experiencing a discussion by joining in wherever one can be found, perhaps in a university seminar, a church or community meeting, or at home.
4 *Practice*: doing the things that discussion leaders do, perhaps one or two at a time separately if not all at once, perhaps for a few moments if not for the whole class period. Try the helpful exercises suggested at the end of this book.
5 *Reflection*: thinking over what was seen, read, experienced and attempted, wondering about its rightness, reformulating it and

resolving on a better try next time. Discipline behaviour to serve educational purpose in classroom circumstance.

With good fortune, the individual teacher will find a colleague or two with whom to share these approaches to learning discussion. Other approaches involving groups of teachers are available from responsible teacher educators, school administrators and educational researchers. Here are examples of helpful approaches, illustrating as well the role of the teacher's fundamental beliefs regarding discussion.

Training programmes

In 'Learning to moderate discussions', Klinzing and Floden (1990) rely on decades of experience with training German teachers for discussion to propose the notion of helping teachers improve by inquiring into and experimenting with their own practice. For this approach the teachers need background knowledge about discussion, analytical ability, and a capacity to generate and to test hypotheses by carrying out actions skilfully – for example, the detailed actions of organizing, structuring and soliciting discussion. To practise discussion the teachers need not just leadership skills but also emotional self-control, patience, frustration tolerance, intellectual versatility, readiness for mutual understanding, and a willingness to give up authority (ibid.: pp. 175–6). Teachers who follow such an approach in a group instead of individually, experience greater improvement for themselves and also contribute significant improvements to our general knowledge of classroom discussion.

The group approach is the essence of Eileen Francis' *Learning to Discuss* (Francis 1986) and *Working Together on Discussion* (Francis and Davidson 1986), an admirable project to spread discussion in Scottish schools. She established a 'discussion development group', in which teachers learned communication skills and group processes through experiential learning of discussion. The teachers committed themselves to a year-long working group in which they learned about discussion, returned to hold discussion in their classroom, and again joined in the discussion group to reflect on their experiences both in their classroom and now in the

group. Through this approach the teachers experienced themselves some of what their students might have been experiencing.

Intervention studies

Intervention studies describe efforts to help practising teachers
improve their discussion leadership. One informative instance is
the six-month effort made by Donna Alvermann and associates
(Alvermann and Hayes 1989) to help five high-school teachers to
change from using recitation to discussion. Their efforts included
conferences with the teacher, observation of the teaching, analysis of the videotaped lessons, joint lesson planning and further
analysis of the intervention. But the efforts were unsuccessful; the
teachers did not shift towards discussion but maintained recitation. The authors realized that in attempting to modify the
teachers' discussion behaviour, they were attempting to modify
the very culture of the classroom, and that the attempted changes
conflicted with the teachers' experiences, beliefs and intuitions
(ibid.: p. 332).

A similar approach was taken by Nate Swift and associates
(Swift and Gooding 1983) in an award-winning study that tried
workshops, practice, observation, audio-taping and conferences
with ten middle-school science teachers who had volunteered to
change their recitation behaviour towards true discussion. The
researchers carefully listened to the teachers' expressed concerns
over content coverage, student motivation and discipline problems. They installed a traffic signal in the classrooms to get the
teachers to slow down their questioning and pause for at least
three seconds in the interaction. Red light, wait! Green light, talk!

GROUP/CLASS

What must the group circumstance be like in order for the class to
hold a discussion? In principle, any class can hold a discussion –
providing only that students and teacher have a question about
the subject matter and a willingness to discuss it. Some classes
discuss better than others, and some classrooms are set up better
for discussion than others. These are matter-of-fact states of

classroom setting and group dynamics. Any class that aspires to discuss must first have formed a community of inquiry.

Community of inquiry

It is the class that discusses, not individual students plus a teacher. The class forms the discussion group. Individuals do not proceed to form into a class as a matter of course, for in some classrooms there remains a collection of individuals instead of a class. And not all classes proceed to form into a discussion group. A class discussion group forms when there is a community of inquiry. Otherwise, the class becomes some other group, forming a different community of other interests, or else the classroom contains a collection of individuals representing disparate interests.

Community of inquiry represents shared interests in discussion. It is formed by communal dispositions and sustained interrelations.

1 *Communal dispositions.* In its character as a group, the discussion class shares some question about the subject matter and some willingness to talk it over within this group and in this classroom. Students may have various questions about different aspects of the subject matter, and correspondingly varying degrees of willingness to talk these over. The class overall experiences questioning about the subject matter and yearning to resolve it through discussion. The greater the communal disposition, the more that the class forms a group for discussion.
2 *Sustained interrelations.* A group does not appear all of a sudden and then disappear. (People who foregather in that way form not a group but some other type of multiple assemblage.) A discussion group is formed of sustained interrelations among members, connecting the people, the work that they do together, and the processes through which they engage together in their common task. Where these are not severally interrelated, community and inquiry are deficient. 'The classroom discussion is a persisting community of query', says Buchler (1954: 10), presupposing earlier achievements, evolv-

ing interests and future obligations. The class that is discussing matter *M* on Wednesday has been discussing some of *A* through *L* on previous days and will be together discussing *O* through *Z* as time goes along.

In the ideal, a discussion group among adults is 'a working group that either lives together communally or meets together often over an extended period of time' (Osinski *et al.* 1972: 58). In either case the discussion group forms a community in the real as well as ideal sense. A class does not live communally but it does meet often and regularly over time. When it forms a discussion group, it is a community of inquiry made up of communal dispositions and sustained interrelations.

Classroom setting

Although there are ideal classroom settings that are conducive to discussion, classrooms are typically not set up for discussion. They are set up for other purposes and processes, and nothing much can be done about that. The classroom setting for discussion is apt not to be ideal.

Research and experience have demonstrated that discussions go better in a small group of five or ten members than in larger groups, and better in groups that are composed by gender, age and ability so as to be cohesive and successful. In addition, the small, well-composed discussion group should have ample time available for an open, unhurried process. They should be comfortably situated, seated closely for ease of eye contact, normal tone of voice and unstrained listening, all in a quiet and pleasant room free of all distraction.

Practice reveals nothing like these conditions. Most classes meet under crowded, pressured and distracting circumstances. Schoolrooms have thirty to forty children in them and college halls a hundred or more. No-one in the class has any say about its size, its composition, its scheduling, its furnishings and surroundings. The furnishings are not comfortable and they may be immovably inflexible; no amelioration or rearrangement may be possible. From the surroundings intrude bells, crowds, messengers, traffic and all manner of distractions. Participants in the discussion have to raise voices, crane necks, twist and strain bodies in order to see and hear one another.

In practice, any class will just have to hold discussion as best as it can under the circumstances in which it finds itself placed. The ideal setting should therefore be forgotten, and all rosy scenarios and prescriptions waived aside. The class should start straightaway into real discussion right where it is at.

Group dynamics

A class discussion incorporates bodies as well as minds, feelings as well as thoughts, irrationality and interpersonality along with intellectual exchange and analysis. These form part of the group atmosphere – and they provoke some of the atmospherics! For example, Eileen Francis (1988) and her discussion development group of committed teachers experienced a series of factors that shaped their processes of discussion, both in their classroom and in their own group:

1 *Boundary*: the divisions between membership and leadership, the limits and rules of task and participation.
2 *Dependency*: reliance on leader and others to initiate and sustain group work, not feeling responsible for the discussion task.
3 *Resonance and resistance*: the excitement and stimulation felt in working together well, or coping with the opposite.
4 *Transfer*: expectations, perceptions and fantasies brought to the discussion from other group settings and experiences including teaching and learning.
5 *Displacement*: assigning to this group, its leader and members, uncomfortable actions and feelings from past group experiences.

This is just one short list of rather familiar items. They illustrate for us some of the influences on discussion stemming from how we see what a group or class is and how it works. The exchange consists not just in the verbal statements and the conceptual propositions they contain, it carries also our perceptions and processes of power and authority, cooperation and rivalry, teaching and studenting, and the rest. These sorts of things seem psychological, even rather personal. Indeed, they are, but not just psychological. They are also social, interpersonal and interactional dynamics animating our discussion.

We as educators should know full well what group dynamics are and how they function in discussion to enhance or to diminish it. To find out about the emotions of teaching and learning, I recommend Arthur Jersild's (1955) classic, *When Teachers Face Themselves*, and books such as *The Emotional Experience of Learning and Teaching* (Salzberger-Wittenberg *et al.* 1983). To learn all about how groups operate, I recommend the authoritative writings of Herbert Thelen (*Dynamics of Groups at Work*, 1954) and the fascinating detailed study of Theodore Mills, *Group Transformation: An Analysis of a Learning Group* (1964). Still better, we might also be able to join a group and experience the dynamics of discussion while reading about it and reflecting on our experience; or, as a second best, we might share the dynamic lessons experienced by the teachers in Francis' discussion group (Francis 1986, 1988; Francis and Davidson 1986).

Group dynamics are not apart from discussion but a part of it. They animate the way we act and talk together. How should we act in discussion? How should we talk? (See Chapters 4 and 5.)

4

HOW TO CONDUCT
A DISCUSSION?

When we ask about the behaviour of people in discussion, we want to know how students and teacher conduct themselves. Regarding the teacher's conduct we are chiefly interested in the pedagogy of discussion, and for students, their participation in discussion. How should the teacher act? How should the students act?

The general principle of pedagogy is to discipline teacher behaviour in favour of educational purpose in classroom circumstance. The case here is class discussion. The pedagogy of discussion is distinct in spirit and act from that of other types of lessons such as recitation. The teacher's behaviour in discussion is far less didactic, directive, controlling and instructional, and more suited to exemplifying and facilitating the discussion.

It is the students who discuss. Accordingly, the teacher's actions must be those that help the students to discuss. The teacher acts to help the students to discuss the question before them, and also to learn how to discuss in general, for other questions and circumstances. In general, the students act in communal address to the discussion question, while the teacher acts to help them to discuss by modelling and maintaining discussion behaviours. Neither party should so conduct themselves as to foil discussion.

We will now apply these general principles to how teacher and students should act during five successive moments or phases of discussion, beginning with (1) preparation for discussion and (2) presentation of the discussion question, moving on to (3) the initial address to the question and through (4) the ensuing exchanges over the question, to (5) the conclusion of the discussion period. We will see that, in principle, students come over time to perform most of the behaviours that the teacher performs. For instance, the students come to exercise leadership functions in the discussion group. It is an essential part of the pedagogy of discussion that the teacher so act as to help the students to learn how to discuss while helping them to discuss the question before them, so that they can join with their fellows to discuss other questions in other circumstances. The first thing everyone must do, and learn to do, is to prepare for discussion.

PREPARATION FOR DISCUSSION

Before entering into the actual discussion period, the teacher prepares for discussion by carefully formulating the discussion question and outline. Students, too, may prepare by wondering about, and/or writing questions about, the previous class activity or other lesson leading to the discussion.

Discussion question

The discussion question is that question which the class will address during the discussion period. It is the question to which the discussion as a whole represents an answer or an answering process. Therefore it has to be a good question, aptly conceived and laboriously formulated. To identify the question, the teacher reflects on the class' engagement over the subject matter, wondering about the matters that follow from or remain from previous class activity, that place the students in a certain position now with respect to the subject matter, and that promise to strengthen the class' engagement or advance its understanding or other learning once discussed. In a word, which question captures the class' present predicament over the subject matter?

The teacher writes this question down, formulating it into a single interrogative sentence – not a word or phrase, not a declarative or imperative sentence. As the teacher thinks about the question to write, several questions actually start coming to mind. One question must be chosen, either from among these or a further candidate that now presents itself. The other questions are jotted down and set aside for the moment. Now that the teacher sets to writing down the chosen question, several variants of this question start flowing from the pen. Some one formulation must be given to the question, and the other versions discarded. What the teacher is preparing is one question, one variant, one formulation, and one version. That and no other will be the question for discussion.

Question outline

With this question clearly in mind and on paper, the teacher sets to making an outline of the discussion, using questions as the items in the outline. Over the long course of conceiving and formulating the discussion question correctly, the teacher has thought of several other questions and has given various forms to them. Now the teacher ponders the discussion question and identifies all the questions surrounding that main question and composing it, such as subsidiary questions, embedded questions, follow-up questions, related questions. These the teacher sorts out, modifies, adds to and selects from, arranging them into a question outline of the discussion. This outline follows the familiar format, save that its entries are questions rather than topical words or sentences:

I   QUESTION
   A   Question
   B   Question
     1   question
     2   question
II QUESTION
   etc.

By way of a related example, this book is outlined in questions. The chapter titles themselves are questions, each chapter bearing on one fundamental question about discussion. The subdivisions within each chapter are sub-questions of the main question. Hence, each chapter answers one question, and each subdivision within chapters answers a particular sub-question about it. Usually the text spells out this question around the major headings, and some of the minor ones. It might be a helpful exercise, for learning both about question outlines and the subject matter of this book, to reconstruct this outline in as much detail as seems fruitful. Next add the answer that the text seems to give to each of the questions. Then compare the question–answers with a colleague's outline of this book. How each reader construes the question–answers is precisely what he and she understands the book to say and to mean. That gives two readers a clear basis on which to discuss this book, by sharing the questions that they think the book is answering, and the answers that they think the book is giving to these questions. Then they can go on to formulate better questions and better answers, thereby forming their knowledge and understanding of discussion.

Returning now to the teacher who is preparing a question outline for the class discussion, we can appreciate that most people may have trouble at first thinking in terms of questions to outline. If the teacher instead starts thinking in terms of topics, he or she need only proceed to formulate the major question about each subtopic, and substitute the interrogative sentence for the topical word in the outline (or attach the question to the topic). If the teacher thinks in terms of statements rather than questions, he or she need only regard the statement as an answer and then construe the question to which it represents an answer, again putting the question in the outline. That will permit the teacher to perceive the other possible answers to that question.

As an elective move, the teacher might then choose to go further and identify the various answers that might be adduced to each of the questions, forming all into a question–answer outline with the special characteristic that several answers are listed under each question. This part of a question outline is not necessary, and may be too complicated for many teachers or purposes. The only essential thing is to outline the questions.

However, where a teacher can proceed to jot down a few answers for at least the discussion question, and perhaps for the main sub-questions, he or she will find it a tremendous practical help in keeping track of the actual discussion process and making sense out of the many exchanges.

With the help of the question outline, the teacher anticipates the range of contributions that students might wind up making in addressing the question. The teacher will be able to recognize the character of what students say, knowing the question that they are addressing and perceiving that their remarks represent this or that sort of answer to that question. The teacher can also see how these contributions interrelate, given the known relations of the questions they answer, and which prior or subsequent question is likely to arise next or be usefully suggested next, given the particular question and answers just addressed. Further, the teacher can tell which possible answers the class as a whole is not identifying, and above all else, which questions the class is neglecting to consider.

As for the length and detail of the outline, the teacher will adjudge these matters as serviceable to purpose and circumstance. None the less, a minimum does seem necessary: an outline has to identify at least three sub-questions and at least four alternative answers to the main question. That minimum will prevent false dichotomies and it will avoid fruitless wrangling over two positions, or mindless recourse to a third position as relief and compromise. Discussion usually requires at least four different viewpoints to be introduced, if not four opposing alternatives. Partly for that reason as well, the question for discussion must not be cast in a form that invites a yes/no or either/or answer. It should not restrict the number of answers but open up to various possible answers (for more details, refer to the section 'Question for discussion' in Chapter 2).

Good, old textbooks on discussion include verbatim outlines illustrating how to prepare a discussion outline. They are lengthy and detailed. One outline takes up five printed pages for the question, 'What should be our policy regarding the teaching of religion in the public schools?' (Sattler and Miller 1954: 329–33). Another takes ten full pages of fine print to outline, 'What should be done to provide adequate medical care for all persons in the

United States?' (McBurney and Hance 1950: 174–84). Perhaps the old-time discussion leaders applied themselves more seriously to the preparation of discussion, or perhaps they did it only once in a while. Whatever the case, an interesting feature of these outlines is that two or three of their five or six main points bear on the problem for discussion. For page after page they specify the problem, defining and analysing it, before mentioning anything about a solution. Their example, although old-fashioned, can still edify us as we prepare for and engage in discussion, by reminding us to emphasize the question before going on to the possible answer.

Another good example of preparation is given in the leader's manual for the Great Books (1991) programme, where people gather to discuss selected books in common. The leader prepares for discussion in five steps:

1 Read the selection at least twice and note your reactions.
2 Identify genuine problems of meaning, writing down twenty or more interpretive questions (What does the author mean by what he or she is saying?).
3 Sort the questions into clusters of one basic question plus related questions.
4 Test the questions by pre-discussing them with someone and revise as called for to be clear, interpretive, interesting, etc.
5 Select one cluster and from it present the basic question for discussion.

The discussion question will be 'a prepared interpretive question to which he or she does not yet have a satisfactory answer, one that the leader is genuinely interested in exploring with the group' (ibid.: p. vii). Although I do not commend the Great Books programme as an exemplary model of discussion, its approach to preparation is a good example for classroom and other discussions, illustrating desirable characteristics even where discussions do not focus on interpretive questions about readings. Namely, there is a question for discussion and it has been well prepared, formulated and related to other questions. The question is one that the group does not have a satisfying answer to, and cares enough about to discuss it.

No doubt but that the burden of preparation falls on the teacher or leader. Yet students too do well to prepare for discussion according to their circumstance. Here are five things they might do.

1 Pupils might merely wonder a bit about the previous class or activity.
2 When given a reading, students too might read it twice, note reactions, and above all jot down the questions that come to their mind about the subject matter.
3 As appropriate, students too might carefully prepare an outline or a list of questions to bring into the discussion, perhaps as an assignment.
4 Going even further, each student might well formulate a candidate question for class discussion, and the class might well spend the discussion period, or part of it, discussing these questions – either in their substance or in their character as candidates for discussion question.
5 Finally, the class itself might prepare and formulate the group's question for discussion. During the first part of a discussion period, the class might deliberate over the question and reformulate it to good purpose.

For more ideas, readers will find entire chapters on using student questions as well as teacher questions in *Questioning and Teaching* (Dillon 1988a). As a useful exercise, readers who are using this book in a course or programme might, in their character as students of discussion, try any of these five ways for preparing for discussion of this very chapter, or other chapters in this book.

From the very outset, then, even during preparation, students as well as the teacher have to act properly. During the ensuing discussion period, students too will come to perform various functions, even leadership functions, as they join in address to the question. First the teacher presents the question.

PRESENTATION OF THE QUESTION

The teacher clearly and physically presents the discussion question to the class. The teacher speaks it aloud and also writes it down on the chalkboard or a poster, or on paper distributed to students or projected on a screen or wall. The physically present question provides a public object for everyone to focus on and refer to as need be during the discussion – especially, as we shall see, at the very beginning.

Having sensibly read the question aloud, the teacher goes on to give the sense of the question. The teacher identifies its terms and their meanings or referents, and tells the import of the question for this class. What is the question asking? Why is it a question for us, now? The teacher might include a summary reference to the previous class discussion or other learning activity, showing how this question arises or follows from it.

The complete presentation of the question takes only a few minutes, perhaps two or three. More time might be spent in presenting a question for a large unit of study or a forthcoming series of discussions. But the presentation should remain short, well prepared and well rehearsed. The teacher doesn't have to fumble around because he or she has already thought these matters through in preparation for the discussion period. The class predicament has taken clear shape in the teacher's mind, and the discussion question has taken clear form on the teacher's paper. The teacher doesn't say three or four versions of the question, or two or three other questions, because the teacher knows full well just exactly what the question for discussion is, and that is the only question that the teacher speaks.

As needed, the teacher might also recall the class to discussion, telling its members that this will be a discussion period, reminding or instructing them as to what discussion is, how to act and talk in it, and how the teacher will help the class to discuss. These explicit matters will ordinarily not arise in every class period but may be needed on occasions when the class first begins its work together, embarks on a new unit or course of study, falters and needs to rally round, and so on.

The presentation ends with an invitation to the class to begin addressing the question. The teacher makes it plain that there stands the question and now begins the class discussion of it. Some student must start speaking to the question, says the teacher, resolutely falling silent and expectantly glancing around the room until some student shall begin to speak.

ADDRESS TO THE QUESTION

At the start of the interchange, the principal task of the teacher is to help the students to address the question. The proper first thing for the class to do is to grasp the question that it is addressing, and then to address the question rather than the answer or solution. Both of these tasks are quite difficult for a group to do. Right at the very start they require disciplined behaviour from the students and steady support from the teacher. For people will act impulsively to bypass the question and start in on the answer.

Presented with a question or problem, a group moves immediately to answer or solution. Almost invariably, the first member to speak states a solution, often interrupting the very statement of the problem. Without realizing it, the group is now at risk for discussion, but the leader can plainly see what is going wrong. The second member to speak is going to criticize or otherwise depart from the first speaker, usually by stating a different solution.

What is happening here that puts discussion at risk? From the very outset, we see a process bearing on solution rather than on problem, on my or his proposal rather than ours, and on advocacy rather than inquiry. Instead of group searching we now face a debate, or an argument, or wrangling over whose position is better. It is next to impossible to introduce a third position, for everyone is already busy taking sides. Even a second position may fail to enter because everyone is busy enough defending or attacking the first and only position so far stated. For instance, if speaker 2 criticizes the first solution, then speaker 1 will be sure to respond in defence. If instead 2 agrees (instead of criticizes), a third speaker will criticize and 1 or 2 will defend. On the other hand, where speaker 2 disagrees by stating a different solution, speakers 1 or 3 will counter it, while 2 or 4 will defend it. Discussion is long gone, chased away from the start.

What is lost in all of this exchange is the question for discussion. Not having focused on the question but moving straight to the solution, the group does not grasp the question that it is supposed to be discussing, and hence it is likely not discussing that question or not discussing at all but doing something else. No-one quite knows what the question is to which speaker 1 proposes an answer, nor in which particular respects of the question that answer might be a good or bad one, or answer 2 better or worse. But that does not stop people from talking about the proposed answer. They readily agree/disagree, criticize/support, attack/defend, advocate/counter it. However, they are not talking about it in the same respects; they agree on various grounds and disagree on disparate grounds. Not only may people be talking at cross-purposes, but they also might not be talking about the question at all but about other matters in respect to which they like or dislike a proposed solution – for instance, the person who proposed it, the problems that it creates, or indeed some other question that it answers (not the discussion question).

Nothing much can be done about this sorry situation once people have got themselves into it. Discussion is not only gone but has never even started, and it can neither be brought back nor started up in this circumstance. I recommend that the teacher or leader take steps to stop the interchange and to help members identify and reflect on what they are doing and how they might go about doing it better next time. Then everyone should just go home or go on to the next lesson; they can have another go at discussion tomorrow.

However, the group can take steps to avoid getting into this mess in the first place. The teacher can help the class to focus on the question. That is, in the first few exchanges the students must talk about the question rather than give their answers to it. The teacher certainly doesn't want to discourage the students from talking, and surely does want to capitalize on their energy and willingness to get going in the discussion. What should they do? What should they talk about? The best advice I know of (from Lasker, 1949) is for people to give their testimony to the problem. They start by saying the following kinds of things:

- *What they know about this question*: their relevant experiences, learnings and the like (not necessarily academic or formal knowledge).
- *What this question means to them*: their interests and attachments to the question, their concerns and troubles over it, their hopes, aspirations, desires respecting it, and the like.

By that means, students launch from their very first words into several essential aspects of discussion. Every one of them can talk about these things, and their talk is genuine and to the point. No-one has to be an expert, figure things out or come up with irrefutable propositions in order to contribute, for anyone can rightly say what they know about this question and what the question means to them. The contributions also interrelate and cumulate in a growing group sense of relation to the question.

Further desirable developments follow. The students begin to form a group understanding of the question they are to discuss and, further, a group agreement to discuss that question. This understanding and agreement builds from the complex of interests and experiences that are being specifically related to the question that stands before the class for all to see (e.g. on the chalkboard). It is to that that the students have turned, not to an answer or onto one another, and they have turned to it as a class or group. The class now is focused on the question. The question becomes an object of group inquiry, one understood and agreed by the class. All of them now sense that they are implicated in this matter and are ready to start pursuing it together.

One additional task might develop. The class group might also reformulate the question as it begins to address it, or the group might reject the question in favour of a preferred question that the group has discovered and formulated in the course of addressing the presented question. That is now the crux of the matter for them, the question that they actually experience about the subject matter and the one they are really willing to discuss. As the class moves along over time and people get more practiced together, the teacher will be helping students to identify the class predicament in relation to the subject matter, and to formulate the question for discussion, as well as presenting, addressing and reformulating it as discussion proceeds.

EXCHANGES OVER THE QUESTION

Throughout the ensuing exchanges over the question, the teacher disciplines as ever his or her behaviour in favour of educational purpose in this classroom circumstance. Here the class is engaged in discussion. Thus the teacher so acts as to help the students to discuss. What do they do? Basically, they participate and they perform needed group functions. They may also misbehave. The students as well as the teacher must try their best to act rightly in discussion, and to forestall or forswear behaviours that would turn them away from discussion.

Participation

To participate in discussion is to join with others in addressing the question. Although literally dozens of behaviours and communication and interaction skills have been identified for discussion, participation comes down to three simple acts: speaking, listening and responding.

Students participate by contributing what they have on the question under discussion (not withholding what they have) and by listening to and responding to what others have to say on the matter (not ignoring it, and not responding to something else). As the students speak, the teacher acts to model and to maintain discussion, chiefly by listening attentively and responding aptly to contributions.

In general, the teacher in discussion does not ask questions, whether to initiate or to sustain an exchange or to respond to a contribution. Instead, the teacher uses a range of non-question moves or alternatives to questioning: various statements, signals, student questions, even silence. These prove to enhance discussion processes, whereas teacher questions foil discussion and turn it into some other group talk. The details of these moves are reserved for the next chapter (Chapter 5) on the language of discussion. There we will get a good sense of how people talk in the exchange; here the topic is how they act.

Just as the group's initial address to the question proves critical to the ensuing process of discussion, so too is the leader's behaviour at two initial 'test-points' of group functioning (Scheidel and Crowell 1979: 150):

1 *After the leader's invitation to begin.* If someone starts to make a contribution and others attend to that speaker and then respond, the test is passed. If not, the leader must not answer

the discussion question but again invite and await contributions, glancing expectantly over the group.

2 *After the first member's contribution.* If the first contribution is a comment, the test for the leader is to avoid being the one who responds to the comment. The leader remains silent and looks invitingly about the group for some other member to volunteer another contribution. The leader must not ask the question, 'What does someone else think of that?' This empty and harmful move keeps the leader in charge, takes away the members' volunteering (whoever talks next is responding to the teacher's question, not proffering an idea of his or her own accord), and appears to invite difference or opposition to the stated view, thus tying the original speaker to that position and now identifying a second speaker with a different one. Similarly, if the first contribution is a question about the substance of the topic, the leader has to make sure that someone else begins the reply. If the question concerns procedure, the leader may clarify or straightforwardly justify the announced proceeding, and then move on.

Thereafter the students continue the interchange and the teacher continues to model and to maintain discussion. Although all manner of tips, rules and prescriptions have been elaborated to guide participation, it seems a straightforward enough affair to speak to the question and to listen and respond to one another. Here is a short list with some good old-fashioned advice to participants (McBurney and Hance 1950: 199–203):

1 *Consider the common good.* Show some concern for the welfare of the group, and work honestly and faithfully towards the group purpose. Be frank and above-board in your conduct, and put all your cards on the table.

2 *Assume your share of group responsibility.* Be as concerned about the success of the discussion as you have a right to expect the leader to be.

3 *Don't think too long before speaking.* Throw your idea into the discussion for what it is worth. Don't be afraid even if you're not sure, but let the group know what you are thinking. Discussion is a process of people thinking out loud.

4 *Contribute objectively.* Be careful against making your contribu-

tions personal issues, involving you in defending your idea, saving face, and feeling resentment over criticism or disagreement.

5 *Listen to understand.* Make an honest attempt to understand the point that a speaker is trying to make, giving your undivided attention, especially if you think you disagree. The best test is to restate the speaker's position in such a way that he accepts your statement as a fair summary of his position.

Leadership functions

A group leader also has to exercise other functions in helping the group to discuss. Endless lists have been drawn up of the things that leaders do. Usually these lists overspecify the behaviours of a leader, detailing many ordinary and commonsense things that people who are not even leaders do. But what functions does an individual perform in his or her character as a group leader? Here is a short, useful list of one set of functions involving the line of thought that the group is in the process of developing (from Scheidel and Crowell 1979: 90–2):

1 *Locating*: Where are we now? The group may need a clear understanding of its present line of thinking. The leader might say, for example, 'Let's see, what are we saying?'

2 *Summarizing*: What have we accomplished? The group needs a clear understanding of the points that have been established or agreed upon. 'Our proposal has three parts – do I have them the way we want them? One part was . . .'.

3 *Opening*: What shall we do next? The group needs a smooth transition to a new aspect of the subject or to the relevant next inquiry. 'Perhaps we are now ready to suggest causes of the problem as we have described it; what might we say is one of the causes operating here?'

4 *Tracking*: How can we all get back on the same line of thought? 'I wonder whether we're getting off the track a little here? We were trying to . . .'.

5 *Pacing*: How can we spend our time where we need it most? 'Just a minute, I wonder whether we're not moving a little too fast here. Could we take a closer look at this one idea about X before we move on?'

Although called management functions, we can see at a glance that these are not acts of telling people what to think and do, but helping the group to manage its exchanges over what to think and do. We can also appreciate that these five functions can be exercised by group members, not just by the leader. For instance, the teacher can help students to provide a summary, and can support students who try to keep the talk on track. On the view that leadership is a group function and not the assigned task of some one individual, all members of the group, at different times and in various respects, can supply the needed leadership.

It is in fact one of the further responsibilities of the teacher to help students in their exercise of leadership functions, along with other functions of discussion groups. The students never become the teacher, to be sure, and the teacher always remains in the discussion and in charge of the class, both to help the students to discuss this topic and to teach them how to discuss topics. Part of this effort will be to foster in students those dispositions, and to guide them towards those behaviours, that enable them to form with their fellows and engage in discussion beyond this class-room. Leadership and management count among those functions that people must exercise in group discussion, and hence need to learn in classroom discussions.

Misbehaviours

People have countless ways of misbehaving in discussion. These inappropriate behaviours foil discussion and turn it into some-thing else. Rather than list them here, some examples are given to show how easy it is to recognize such behaviour. We can see clearly that they just don't belong in discussion because they violate basic principles of discussion (see Chapter 1). They belong somewhere else.

A range of misbehaviours violates the moral culture of group discussion (Bridges 1979). People violate peaceableness by inter-rupting or shouting down opinions they dislike; they violate truthfulness by remaining silent, reticent, covert; they violate reasonableness by refusing to listen or to be influenced by reason and evidence; and so on.

Other misbehaviours are 'enemies of open discussion' (Bridges

1979), violating the various dimensions of openness. Some of these behaviours are more subtle than heavy-handed authoritarian devices but they are no less inimical. They include kindliness, or protecting certain members from the truth because it might hurt them or they might not handle it well; loyalty to institution, faith, cause or person instead of to the purposes of inquiry; pursuit of consensus instead of truth; making sure that people get it right or come to the right conclusion; making it easy for anxious members to contribute, instead of maintaining the group task and standards for the exploration of problems and opinions in the search for understanding.

Misbehaviours violate the unspoken contract of group members who gather for serious problem solving (Phillips *et al.* 1979: 144–5). Instead of engaging in group problem solving, the misbehaving member uses the group to solve personal and emotional problems, to waste time, to make idle chatter, to make friends and do combat with enemies, to be truculent, to polarize the group, to attack members, to demand his or her way and concede nothing to others.

Misbehaviour exploits the free and open exchange of discussion for purposes of proselytizing, confounding, diverting, sensationalizing, displaying erudition, winning polemical victories, 'and in general putting forward a false or partial self in spurious exchange for the authentic self-disclosures and self-commitments offered by the genuine participants in the discussion' (Paterson 1970: 48).

Advocacy is misbehaviour in discussion. Debate is misbehaviour. Persuasion and conversation are misbehaviours.

Just as it is the special responsibility of the teacher to be a model of exemplary discussion behaviour, so also must the teacher act as a steady spoiler of all behaviours that foil discussion. Students are expected to join the teacher in deflecting and correcting all moves to turn the class away from communal inquiry, reflective thinking, deliberation and the like.

CONCLUSION OF THE DISCUSSION PERIOD

At some point towards the end of the period or class hour, the teacher must act to draw discussion to a close. The two major acts are to summarize the discussion and to identify the question remaining. The teacher also acts, as before, to help students to work out for themselves the summaries and questions.

Summary

In a few well-chosen sentences having to be composed fairly on the spot, the teacher offers a summary of the discussion period, reflecting the major points and especially the present status of the group in relation to the matter discussed.

Summaries are difficult to compose. They are short and they must be accurate. The teacher must especially discipline self against adding to the group's development or changing it in any way, even for the better. What the teacher is trying to do is not to improve, clarify or even shape the group's idea or stance but to help the group grasp just what it has come to understand or to resolve about the topic. When the teacher acts wrongly to give shape to the group's idea, the summary dismisses the group's actual development, prevents the group from grasping its actual understanding of the topic, and encourages the group to depend on the teacher to shape up its ideas next time. The mistaken summary may also provoke correction and needless further exchange at just the moment when exchanges should cease and other activities should begin, such as summary and reflection. The teacher should also act to help students to formulate the group summary. For instance, the final five minutes of a period might be reserved for students to reflect and synthesize, formulate and present the summary.

No discussion is required to come to a conclusion, although all discussions must come to a close. And while matters might not be resolved to satisfaction during a single session, they could be, and they eventually will come to some resolution. To test for resolution of the question, the Great Books (1991) programme has an interesting procedure. The discussion question in this programme always bears on interpretation of a reading done in common. Towards the end of the two-hour session, the leader:

- repeats the question;
- calls on members to repeat the answers they remember hearing;

- checks if anyone in the group has an answer that has not yet been repeated, or discussed in the first place;
- has members compose their final answer;
- asks members to identify the ideas (contributions) from the discussion that led them to develop their thinking, change their mind, and form their final answer.

To these I would add for a classroom circumstance, identifying what is left of the question or reading to discuss, and formulating the new or next question for discussion.

Question remaining

Whether the presented question has been resolved or not, the teacher must act to identify the present question facing the group. That question follows immediately from the summary.

If the group has resolved the discussion question, a new question will arise on the very grounds of that resolution. In technical terms, the resolution forms a question–answer proposition that serves in turn as the presupposition giving rise to a subsequent question (see Dillon, 1990, for how questions work). If the group has not resolved the question, it will have clarified or otherwise settled selected aspects of it, and a new question has to be formed out of the aspects not resolved, plus further matters likely adduced to the question in the course of discussing it. In either case, the teacher identifies the question remaining for the class. As ever, the teacher also invites and helps students to identify for themselves their own individual and class questions.

This new question can in turn serve as the focus of the next discussion, or for suitable assignments and other learning activities in class. In that way, the question for discussion sensibly arises out of the class' previous engagement with the subject matter, focuses the class' present engagement, and sensibly directs its upcoming engagements.

5

HOW TO TALK
IN DISCUSSION?

When we ask about the language of discussion, we want to know the ways that people should talk as appropriate to the discussion process. What are their choices among different ways of talking, and what effects do their choices have on the processes of discussion?

In principle, students should talk in address to the discussion question and in response to one another's contributions over it. The teacher's talk should help the students to talk this way, viz. to discuss. Accordingly, the teacher should avoid putting questions to students, and instead choose to use various *alternatives to questioning* – statements, signals, silences, student questions. These prove to enhance the processes of discussion. They help students to contribute over the question and to respond to developing contributions, while they also model for students exemplary discussion behaviour. That is the way that people should talk in discussion.

TYPES OF TALK

What are the different kinds of things that people might say in discussion? At some point, a given speaker will be making a contribution on the question, stating his or her view of the matter being discussed at that point. What are the others to say next? In general terms, they have four broad choices, each with several specifics to choose from. They can:

1 Ask a *question* about what the speaker has said.
2 Make a *statement* in relation to what the speaker has just said.
3 Give a *signal* of receiving what the speaker is saying.
4 Maintain an attentive *silence*.

Although any participant can say these things, the teacher's lead and example are particularly helpful to students. From the pedagogical viewpoint, the choice of how to talk is disciplined in favour of educational purpose in classroom circumstance. What shall the teacher say that will help the students to discuss, in the twin senses of fostering the discussion and fostering appropriate discussion behaviour in students? On that view, a critical distinction must be drawn between teacher and student questions, giving in all these five broad choices: teacher questions, student questions, statements, signals and silences.

For each of these five choices we will first state the principle of using it and describe various specific kinds of talk of that type. We will relate some of its rationale and provide a few illustrations and examples drawn from classroom transcripts and research studies. Interested readers will find extensive treatments of these points in books by Dillon (1988a, 1990).

Teacher questions

The principle of teacher questioning during discussion runs: *Do not put questions to students during a discussion.* I explicitly recommend against questioning by the teacher. Teacher questions will foil discussion processes, turning the class into some other group talk much like recitation. Teacher questions do not stimulate student thinking and they do not encourage participation. They depress student thought and talk.

The teacher can foster discussion processes by actively using *non*-questioning alternatives – statements, signals, silences and student questions. These alternatives do stimulate student thinking and they do encourage student participation. They also model for students the appropriate ways of talking during a discussion.

1 *Discussion question.* Pose the question for discussion. Ideally, this is the sole question that the teacher should pose. This one question is sufficient for the hour's discussion.
2 *Self-perplexing questions.* Raise only the questions that perplex you. Do not ask questions that do not perplex you. The teacher might permissibly raise one, or perhaps two, genuinely self-perplexing questions during the discussion. More to the point are the questions that perplexed students raise in genuine wonderment over the subject matter.
3 *Questions to students.* Put no questions at all to students. Do not ask questions but instead use alternatives to questioning. For instance, state your thought to the student.

Statements

The principle of making a statement (instead of asking a question, for example) runs: *State your selected thought in relation to what the speaker has said.* The generic exchange goes as follows:

- Speaker – contribution on the question.
- Teacher or student – statement related to contribution.
- Speaker – response to statement.

Contrary to what might be obvious, people do respond to statements. Questions are not the only utterances to which people respond, while seeking or getting a response is not the defining characteristic of questions but a common characteristic of statements as well. Moreover, student responses to teacher statements are longer and more complex than their answers to teacher questions.

A good illustration from research is the series of studies by David and Heather Wood of Nottingham, England, summarized in 'Questioning versus student initiative' (Wood and Wood 1988). Initiative describes the proportion of child responses that are marked by unsolicited, voluntary material such as elaborated answers, spontaneous contributions, ideas and questions asked by the child. In every case studied – toddlers at home, children in preschool, pupils in primary school and students in secondary school – the children responded at greater length and with greater initiative to statements than to questions. For example, in the case of secondary classes, student initiative was twice as great for statements as for questions (91 *vs* 45 per cent), while for primary pupils it was three times greater (66 *vs* 18 per cent). The children not only talked far more, but they also talked far better in response to statements, going beyond to elaborate, to volunteer contributions and ideas, and to ask questions themselves.

Here are six kinds of statements that teacher and students might make in discussion. When some speaker has just made a contribution, the next speaker can make a declarative statement, a reflective restatement, a statement of mind, a statement of interest, a speaker referral, or a self-report.

1 *Declarative statement: State the (pre-question) thought that occurs to you as a result of what the speaker has just been saying.* For a generic example, the speaker has just stated that something is the case: 'X is the case'. The thought occurs to you that Y is the case. So you say to the speaker: 'Y is the case'. For a specific example, in transcript 4 at the end of the book, a student has just said that two viewpoints are incompatible, and the teacher says: 'I don't think they're totally incompatible, the things you're saying. I just think there are two different ways of looking at them' (exchange 1a).

Your statement need not be the opposite of what the speaker has said; the two statements might be complementary instead of opposed. For instance, the speaker might say, 'Roses are red', and you might declare, 'Violets are blue'. Your statement need not be complementary either, or anything else – all it has to be is *informative of your thought* in relation to what the speaker has been saying. Now the speaker has the benefit of your thought in relation to his or hers, and the two of you can discuss them.

It is difficult for people straightforwardly to declare the thought that is in their mind; they tend to veil it. Teachers especially tend to ask a question instead of stating their thought. To help the teacher discipline behaviour against this impulse, I recommend stating the *pre*-question *thought* – that is, the thought that comes to mind immediately before the question that comes to the lips. An easy way to do this is to go ahead and answer your own question. When the question comes to mind, keep the question quiet but *answer it aloud*. By that means you will be declaring your thought to the speaker instead of requiring the speaker to figure out which of your thoughts he is supposed to declare; and the speaker will have the direct and immediate benefit of your thought in relation to his.

2 *Reflective restatement: State your understanding of what the speaker has just said, giving your sense of it in one economical and exact sentence.* There are two basic ways to restate the speaker's contribution:

- *Repeat it* – the speaker says, 'X is the case'. You say, 'X is the case'.
- *Summarize or characterize it* – the student speaks various letters from A to Z, in some jumbled order. You say, 'The alphabet is the case, or maybe some jumble of letters'.

The speaker will respond with something like, 'Right', or 'Well, what I meant was . . .', in either case going on to enhance his or her original contribution by extending and improving it. For example, in Mr T's discussion on European history (transcript 2 at the end of book), Diane is speaking about Louis XIV's reasons for persecuting the Huguenots, and the teacher characterizes her contribution.

> *Mr T*: So you feel that he was justified in what he was doing, as far as he was concerned – he could justify it to himself.
> *Diane*: Yeah, he could justify it to himself. But then, . . . [continues for 11 seconds].

In Mr S's discussion about sexual topics in the students' home life (transcript 3), Marilyn is speaking about her family's way of talking about sex. The teacher reflects her statement and she elaborates, connecting her contribution with that of a previous speaker (exchange 14a):

> *Mr S*: You do this all together.
> *Marilyn*: Yeah, my mother and father and all the rest of us. And just like he said, . . . [continues for 21 seconds].

Other reflective statements used by this teacher begin with the phrase, 'So you're saying that . . .' e.g. 'So you're saying that your parents never sat you down and talked about sex' (exchange 3a). That is one helpful way of starting a restatement – providing, of course, you don't try to change what the speaker has been saying.

Reflective restatements may be hard to make, given the impulse to substitute our own thought for the speaker's, or given the habit of not listening in the first place to what someone else is saying. By making such a restatement, the teacher signals to everyone in the room the importance of attending and listening to the speaker, and of getting the speaker's meaning right before reacting to it. A reflective restatement permits the speaker – and other participants – to infer that what he or she thinks and says *matters*. It confirms the speaker in the effort to contribute, assures him or her of a hearing, and makes a public possession of a private meaning. The result is to encourage participation and to facilitate discussion of actual rather than imaginary meanings.

3 *Statement of mind: Describe in truth the state of your mind, and none other, in relation to what the speaker has just been saying.* A speaker has just said that X is the case. Your mind is in some kind of state, let us say that it is square. You so inform the speaker: 'My mind is square about what you're saying.' If you are confused, state your confusion; if you don't understand, state that which you do not understand. If you understand the speaker's point but disagree with it, say so. For example, Mr T (transcript 2) says, 'OK, I can see where you're coming from, but I don't know if I can totally agree with that.' Or when agreeable: 'OK, I'll go along with that.' If, however, you are distracted or in a muddled state, speak your state of mind, saying something like, 'I was thinking about something else just then.' The key is to describe your state of mind, and none other. Then the speaker gets to respond to your true state of mind and you get truly involved in the exchange. Such a statement exemplifies the discussion norm of speaking the truth of your mind, and it demonstrates against the social norm of sitting there and pretending.

4 *Statement of interest: State whatever it is that you are interested in*

hearing further about what the speaker has just been saying. A student says that X is the case. You are interested in aspect Y about X. You say: 'I'm interested in hearing Y about X.' If you'd like to hear more of the speaker's views on that, say: 'I'd like to hear more of your views on that.' Interested in a definition, say: 'I notice you keep stressing X, and I'd be interested in your definition of it.' Needing an example, say: 'It would help me to understand better if I had an example of X.' Of course, if you are not interested in these things you harm discussion by stating an interest in them.

5 *Speaker referral: State the relation between what the speaker has just said and what a previous speaker has said, referring one speaker to another.* Speaker 1 has said that X is the case. Later speaker 2 says that anti-X is the case. You say to speaker 2: 'So you're saying anti-X and speaker 1 is saying X, the opposite.' Then the two speakers can examine their contributions for any relation they might have and go on to discuss them. For example, in Mr T's history discussion, (transcript 2), the teacher first refers students to what Marty said, then refers Marty to what Sean says:

> *Mr T*: All right, Marty raised an interesting point just a few seconds ago. He said that X is the case.
> *Sean*: I think Marty was wrong, because even though X, Y is still the case today.
> *Mr T*: All right, so he's totally disagreeing with what you had to say, Marty.
> *Marty*: Yeah, well – No, he brought up a good point . . . But what I'm saying is . . .

The teacher might refer the speaker to another student, or to the speaker him/herself ('Like you were saying, Pam, X is the case') or various speakers can be referred to the present speaker and to one another:

> OK. I think, ah, we can go backwards to Marilyn's point and take off from that a bit. She said – and I think that some of you are agreeing with her – that X is the case. But Stacey said, and I think that Bonnie's saying the same thing, X is a case of Y.

Students, too, can choose to talk this way, making a speaker referral or any of the other types of statements identified here. For example, the transcribed excerpt of Mr W's discussion on parent–child relations (transcript 4) begins and ends with speaker referrals by Regina. 'I don't see what Paul and Steve said as two separate ideas', she begins (exchange 1b), and she ends the episode by saying, 'I think he has a point of view or whatever, but I think, taking from what Chris said, that . . . And just like he said, . . .' (exchange 10b).

6 *Self report: Give an account of your own status (knowledge, experience, feeling) regarding the matter at hand.* Some speaker has just finished saying, 'X is the case with me.' You say, 'With me, the case is . . .'. In response, another speaker is likely to say, 'That's the case with me, too' or 'See, and in my case, . . .'. For example, at a sensitive point in the discussion about sex in homelife (transcript 3), the teacher, Mr S, makes the mistake of asking Larry directly about witnessing affection between his parents, and Larry evades the question with a comment that produces nervous laughter from the class. So Mr S moves to give an account of the case with him. Larry then responds in kind, and so does Marilyn (exchange 13a):

> *Mr S*: Right. So quickly, one problem I know I have when I think about this question, I can't ever imagine my parents having sex, or whatever. But the thing is, you know, at least the kids – my parents had 10 kids, so I know they went to bed together at least 10 times, you know . . . [laughter] . . . You know, but I still have this trouble connecting that – the reality.
> *Larry*: Yeah, I have that trouble too. I just couldn't . . . [continues for 11 seconds].
> *Marilyn*: In our family, you know we have something like, . . . [continues for 12 seconds].

Here after the teacher's account we see two responses, by students of different sexes, both responses speaking to the topic, in the appropriate manner, and at considerable length.

Reporting need not be a personal revelation about intimate matters, but may concern knowledge and experience about academic and other matters that are under discussion. I once heard a wonderful account from a teacher who was being amazed by student opinions regarding marriage ceremonies:

> Well, that's good, I'm glad to hear some of these things. 'Cause, see, I've lived in my own little world here for so many years, and I don't run into a lot of people that would have a differing opinion from what I have. So that's why I always tell you people that you got about 30 good ideas in here against one of mine, and that's why I like to discuss things with you.

That reporting of self surely encourages the discussion of this and any other subject matter, and models for students an exemplary disposition towards discussion generally.

Student questions

Ensure that a student asks a question in relation to what the speaker has just been saying. This alternative seems odd – a question from a student instead of from the teacher – but it is a well-grounded choice. The student's question enhances the student's cognitive, affective and expressive processes. In itself the student's question instantiates inquiry and it initiates interchange. To ask a question is also to exhibit a complex of active dynamics by contrast to the passive, dependent, reactive dynamics of answering a teacher question. Moreover, students' responses to questions from other students are longer and more complex than to teacher questions. For instance, in first-grade classrooms, the greater part of children's responses to teacher questions were found to consist of one or two words, compared to six and more words in response to questions from other children (Mishler 1978). Furthermore, no other event better portends learning that does a question arising to a child's mind. It is the perfect opening for teaching to enter and for learning to follow in answer. It is through our own questioning that we start to search, and through our own answering that we come to know. Thus on all counts, student questions are desirable for discussion.

As before, the exchange will have begun with some speaker's contribution on the matter being discussed at that point. The teacher may then choose to provide for the speaker's question, for another participant's question, or for the class' question. In each case, the teacher goes on to sustain the question once asked. Thus instead of asking a question, the teacher provides that a student ask a question; and instead of answering the question, the teacher sustains the asking of the question. The generic exchange goes as follows:

- Speaker – contribution.
- Teacher – provides for student question.
- Student – question.
- Teacher – sustains student question.
- Student – discussion of question.

There are endless detailed ways of making these generic moves. In one example, in Mr P's discussion of multiple-personality (transcript 5), the teacher recognizes a student question, asks that it be repeated, praises it, repeats it, supplies background information to it, and again restates it, offering the student question for class discussion (exchange 16a):

> *Duane*: Wouldn't she gain another personality?
> *Mr P*: How do you know – that's a good question – how do you know she wouldn't gain another personality? You got rid of Black and White; you got Jane left; how do you know she wouldn't get another one?

This is but one individual instance of one way of using student questions in discussion, selected from a transcript at the end of this book. There are not many good examples available because not many student questions are ever heard in classrooms. Details of the pedagogy of student questions are found in *Questioning and Teaching* (Dillon 1988a).

1 *Speaker's question: Ensure that the speaker formulates a question about what he or she has just said or is struggling to think and to say.* A speaker has just said, 'Something is the case, I just don't know.' You say, for example, 'Relax for a minute and think about the question that's still bothering you about that.' In response, the speaker comes up with the question, 'Is X the case?' The teacher then acts to sustain the question, saying, for example, 'You're wondering if X is the case. Good question.' In

that way the speaker who is struggling to think and say something gets help with identifying and formulating the matter that is confused in his or her mind. Once the question becomes clear, the speaker can pursue it, often starting to work out the answer in the same breath as speaking the question. Thus the speaker achieves the thought that he or she was fruitlessly trying to express, or else delivers a new and perplexing question for everyone to consider. Either one is a fruitful contribution to discussion.

2 *Participant's question: Ensure that another participant formulates a question about the speaker's contribution or the matter under discussion.* The speaker has just said that something is the case. You say, for example, 'Let's take a minute to hear the question that somebody in here might be thinking about that.' In response some participant says, 'Is X the case?' and the teacher moves as before to sustain the question, saying, for example, 'You're wondering if X is the case. Good question.'

3 *Group question: Ensure that the group formulates the question that now appears at issue in the discussion.* Some speaker has conclusively said that X is the case, or several speakers have just concluded that something is the case, X, Y or Z. At this juncture, the teacher moves to provide that the question for discussion be identified and formulated by the students. For example, 'Maybe it's time now to hear a few suggestions as to the kind of questions we should be asking now, given everything that has been said up to this point.' Some student will come up with, 'Is X the case?' and the teacher again moves to sustain the question by saying, for example, 'One question we might discuss now is whether X is the case. Interesting question.' In that way the teacher acts to help students to identify and formulate questions, to interconnect them in a sequence of inquiry, and to join together in deliberating among compelling issues, determining which one they should discuss. The result is a powerful question for discussion, one that arises from the class' own felt predicament over the subject matter, and one that they are not only asking but also choosing to discuss.

Signals

Signal your reception of what the speaker is saying, without yourself taking or holding the floor. Signals include fillers or verbal encouragers, phatics or quiet exclamations, and passing the turn at talk to another speaker. These are modest devices with substantial functions. They encourage the speaker on, and they open the floor for further participation, all the while giving the teacher something to say or do without actually taking a turn at talk or holding the floor.

1 *Phatics: Uttering a brief phrase, quietly exclaim feeling in reaction to what the speaker has just finished saying.* When the speaker has said that X is the case, you exclaim, for example, 'Oh, X is so nice.' The speaker will then say more about X or go on to say that Y is the case, too. The phrasing of phatics depends on local language usage. You might say 'lovely, wonderful, amazing, interesting, awful', or 'gracious, no, well, really, you don't say'. Although modest in themselves, phatics have substantial effects on discussion. In studies at various school levels, the teacher's use of phatics enhanced the length and initiative of children's responses far more so than questions did, whether open or closed questions. (Initiative describes elaborations, voluntary contributions, ideas and questions from the child.) For instance, preschool children responded to two-choice questions with an average of 2.7 words and 28 per cent initiative; to wh-questions with 3.4 words and 32 per cent initiative; while to phatics their responses averaged 4.6 words and 57 per cent initiative (Wood and Wood 1983).
2 *Fillers: Emitting some word or sound, indicate attentive interest in what the speaker has said or is in process of saying.* When the speaker says that X is the case, you emit, for example, 'Mm-humm'. The speaker will continue about X or go on to say that Y is the case, too. Fillers are normal conversational devices, sometimes called backchannel feedback, for signalling reception: 'Mm-humm, uh-huh, mm, hunh, yes, yeah, I see/understand, fine, right, OK.' People respond positively to these modest indicators. For instance, in employment interviews (McComb and Jablin 1984), the average response to fillers was

found to be an additional six seconds of talk by the inter-
viewee, and a higher rating of the interviewer's empathy and
the communication process in the interview. And in Mr W's
discussion class (transcript 4), we can hear the teacher's
'um-hm' smack in the middle of Regina's 83 second long
contribution (exchange 1b).

3 *Pass: By gesture or word, pass the next turn at talk to another
speaker.* Speaker 1 says that X is the case. You pass – for
example, by saying, 'Go ahead, Speaker 2.' Speaker 2 says that
Y is the case. The teacher might pass to a volunteer by naming
the student or by nodding, waving or smiling at him or her. A
given student who is dominant in the exchange will also find
occasion to pass the turn at talk to some other student.

Silences

Say nothing at all. But do positively maintain silence, remaining
attentive, appreciative and expectant of forthcoming contributions. Silence is either deliberate or non-deliberate. Only deliberate silence is a discussion behaviour. Non-deliberate silence is
trouble for discussion.

1 *Deliberate silence: Say nothing at all but maintain a deliberate,
appreciative silence for 3–5 seconds until the original speaker
resumes or another speaker enters in.* A speaker has just said that
X is the case. You maintain an appreciative, attentive silence – a
quite noticeable pause. After a few seconds the speaker
resumes to say more about X or another speaker enters in to say
that Y is the case, too.

Deliberate silence is the simplest and one of the most
powerful moves that the teacher can make in facilitating
student discussion. It is also the hardest of all for the teacher to
do. To help the teacher to maintain this behaviour in face of all
impulses to talk, I recommend singing 'Baa, baa, black sheep'
while making correlated body movements in support. The
generic exchange goes as follows.

Speaker 1:	X is the case.
Teacher:	['Baa, baa, black sheep have you any wool?'

	Nod, nod to speaker hoping he has more wool.]
Speaker 1:	And Y, too, come to think about it.
Teacher:	['Yes sir, yes sir Three bags full.' Nod, nod, holding for three seconds.]
Speaker 2 or 1:	But not Z – Z isn't the case.
Teacher:	['One for my master, One for my dame, One for the little boy Who lives down the lane.' Look at the speaker, Look at a girl, Look at a boy, Look down the row.]
Speaker 2 or 1:	Z is not the case here because . . .

Odd though it may seem, such silence is a positive teacher behaviour and students respond positively to it. Numerous studies on teacher 'wait-time' and pausing have demonstrated the remarkably positive effects on student cognition and expression. From reviewing these studies, Ken Tobin (1987) concludes that when the teacher maintains silence or wait-time for at least three seconds after a student contribution, student participation increases – in overall student talk-time, number of words and utterances spoken, length of utterances, student-initiated discourse, and student–student interactions. For instance, the pioneering studies by Mary Budd Rowe (1974) showed that as teacher wait-time increased from one to three seconds, student response increased from 7 to 28 words on average, and the number of unsolicited responses rose from 3 to 37. As for cognitive processes, the use of teacher wait-time also results in more complex student responses, higher cognitive level responses, more alternative explanations, and more student questions (Tobin 1987). For example, the average number of inference responses increased from 6 to 14, speculative responses from 2 to 11, and student questions from 4 to 18 (Rowe 1974). These are precisely the kind of cognitive and expressive processes desirable in class discussion.

The teacher's silence also models exemplary discussion behaviour. It models due attentiveness and appreciative listening until such time as a participant shall have delivered him or herself of an entire thought – not just a phrase or a sentence or two. To speak up at the first pause or first flawed phrase is to grab the floor and to dismiss the speaker. It is no less an interruption than when someone is speaking. Indeed, someone *is* speaking – and thinking, too. When the student has ostensibly finished speaking, the teacher should maintain deliberate silence to foster the further talk and thought that is in the process of coming forth.

2 *Non-deliberate silence: You'd better figure out something to do.* Non-deliberate silence is not of the teacher's choosing and acting, and describes a situation in which no known and good purpose is being served. Confusion and trouble may be surfacing or events and people are suspended while the teacher is silent for want of speech and action. The teacher must make a decision as to what to say and do.

PROCESSES OF DISCUSSION

How do these different choices of talk affect the processes of discussion? In particular, what are the effects of the teacher's use of questions by contrast to the non-question alternatives, i.e. the various statements, signals, silences and student questions? In general, teacher questions can be seen to foil discussion, whereas the use of non-question alternatives fosters discussion.

These contrasting effects will be examined in six different cases of discussion, three at the secondary level of school and three at primary and preschool levels (the first three from the USA, the other three from England, Canada and New Zealand). First the three high-school discussions will be examined, next the three with younger children, and then the general case with discussion will be summarized and finally contrasted with recitation. Interested readers will find an extensive review of research studies on this issue in *The Practice of Questioning* (Dillon 1990).

The three high-school classes are instances of different kinds of discussion, thus affording even within this set of cases a useful series of contrasts. They are not merely three different discussions but discussions of three different kinds:

- an 'informational' discussion on sexuality in early homelife, conducted by Mr S (transcript 3 at the end of the book);
- a 'dialectical' discussion on changing child–parent relations, by Mr W (transcript 4);
- a 'problematical' discussion of multiple personality, by Mr P's class (transcript 5).

In each case the transcript represents a ten-minute episode randomly selected for analysis from the hour's discussion. The three discussions figure in a larger case study of how questions foil discussion (Dillon 1985). The classification of these discussions is by Thomas Roby (1988), one of a group of researchers who independently studied these same cases in a multidisciplinary project reported in *Questioning and Discussion* (Dillon 1988b).

Informational discussion

In his senior Marriage class in the final year of secondary school, Mr S (transcript 3) is conducting in a sensitive way a discussion on a rich but touchy subject: sexuality in the students' early homelife. Most of his twenty-four students of both sexes are non-white, and the class is seated in the traditional rectangle with the teacher in front, on a high stool.

Although the lesson proceeds well enough, Mr S, like many other teachers, has his share of disciplinary episodes, public-address system announcements, and other interruptions. Interestingly enough, despite the fragility of public discussion about these matters, a messenger interruption does not disjoint the discussion (exchange 22a).

Mr S wishes to hear and to understand what students say, for that is essential to the kind of discussion he proposes. Here is how he begins the hour:

> Today we want to spend the time sharing the kinds of things that we can remember going on in our family during our childhood. Now the goal here is to help us

understand, that as we begin to recall what went on during our childhood, we might have a better insight into why we are the way we are today . . . And again, let's proceed or keep in the back of our mind that we're also working on how to disclose ourselves to someone else. We're also continuing to learn how to divulge information, and share.

Beyond clarifying one's own present feelings as learned from childhood experiences, Mr S continues, one of the purposes of the discussion is to discover which attitudes and behaviours one might wish to change, and which to pass on to one's children.

In favour of this kind of discussion, Mr S regularly speaks to his students in declarative sentences. The statements summarize in an economical way what the student has just said, or otherwise express Mr S's understanding of the student's meaning or experience. The effect is to encourage discussion. But his occasional questions have the contrary effect. The transcribed episode illustrates these contrasting effects in exchanges with six students.

Larry. Larry opens with some clarifying questions (student questions) and successively longer contributions. Mr S makes the 'reflective statement', 'It wasn't that strict' (exchange 9a). Before that statement, Larry had spoken for 9 seconds, and now he elaborates for a further 13 seconds. Next the teacher asks a question and Larry responds for only 3 seconds. A further question brings a response which evokes class laughter (exchange 12b). Then the teacher discloses something of himself ('self report') and Larry responds at some length that he too has that trouble (exchange 13b).

Marilyn. Next Marilyn volunteers a 12-second contribution and Mr S utters, 'You do this all together' (exchange 14a). Marilyn continues at twice the length as before, moreover connecting her remarks with those of Larry some eight or nine exchanges back. Then the teacher asks a question and we hear her meagre 'um-hm'. Next he offers an interpretive statement: 'I don't know, you seem to feel good about that.' This is the interesting result: Marilyn expounds on her feeling good about that, whereupon

Larry enters in to say that he too thinks that is good, and he too expounds (exchange 16c).

However, after these fruitful exchanges with Larry and Marilyn, Mr S has two exchanges of another kind, produced by his questions about what a student has just said:

Shawn. She is exploring something she doesn't understand (exchange 21b) and, after an external interruption and the teacher's apology, she expansively continues, revealing that her mother told her about sex when she was eight years old (exchange 22b). Now Mr S asks her a question, then another. Shawn's responses drop abruptly and the last produces class laughter (exchange 24b).

Girl. Another girl then volunteers to say that she too can talk with her mother about sex, even about this class. Mr S's interest is alerted and he asks the girl a question, then another. Again the responses diminish and provoke class laughter (exchange 26b).

Sharee. Sharee follows with an expansive contribution which diminishes in response to the teacher's question, then recovers when he states, 'OK, so you're saying they're not so willing to listen or hear your story' (exchange 28a).

Shan. Finally, Shan enters in and no questions are asked. She refers to Shawn's contribution nine or ten exchanges back and speaks at length but somewhat confusedly. The teacher offers a summary interpretation and Shan is able to clarify what she means (exchange 29b).

One way of summarizing the contrast between questions and alternatives in Mr S's class is to note that the students' responses to statements were significantly more expansive, in four ways.

1 Overall, students responded for an average of 8 seconds to Mr S's questions, but 13 seconds to his statements.
2 An individual student's successive contributions were enhanced by the teacher's statements, then abruptly diminished by the questions. Larry's contributions fell from 10 seconds to 3 in response to a question, and Marilyn's from 21 to 1 second; while contributions by Shawn, an unnamed girl and Sharee

dropped from 16 to 3 seconds, 5 to 2 seconds, and 26 to 11 seconds as each answered questions.

3 Other students joined the original respondent in discussion after teacher statements. By contrast, questions involved only a single respondent.

4 The statement-exchanges produced student references to one another's contributions, thereby continuing and deepening discussion. By contrast, the question-exchanges in several cases produced class laughter, thereby disrupting and relieving the discussion.

Dialectical discussion

Mr W's class (transcript 4) offers a second illustration, in contrasting circumstances. Compared to Mr S, Mr W has a large class (41 *vs* 24 students), all but a few of whom are white students, compared with all but a few black students in Mr S's class. The two teachers take the same proportion of turns at talk (42 and 45 per cent), but the pace is more leisurely in Mr W's class – he intervenes only once a minute, compared to three times a minute for Mr S. Everyone in Mr W's class speaks at length, far longer than in the other classes. None the less, the students in both classes respond still more expansively to the teachers' statements than to their questions.

The lesson bears on changes in society from past to present times. The students have a worksheet listing various aspects of society, on which they were to have written examples of changes. Mr W asks them to take out their worksheets: 'We'll use them as the basis for our discussion today.' He goes on to say:

> I'd just like you to volunteer those examples of change that you've been able to come up with, try to explain why, how you see it changed from the past to the present, and we'll try to analyse that in the same way that we have the rest of our society, some of the examples that I gave, like the influence of electronic media.

In the transcribed episode, the aspect at issue is changes in parent-child authority relations.

As the lesson progresses, the teacher praises the students'

contributions (exchanges 3a, 5a), makes connections among them by name (exchanges 1a, 8a, 10a), and asks discussion-like questions: Why do you think? (exchange 2a), How do you mean? (exchange 6a) and the interesting, How to do X and maintain an apparent anti-X, Y? (exchange 8a). The students as well as the teacher speak at considerable length. Yet overall the students respond at nearly three times the length to Mr W's statements as to his questions (40 *vs* 15 seconds).

Regina's initial contribution of 83 seconds diminishes to 39 and 1 second in response to questions, then rises to 23 seconds after a statement. Student talk continues to increase, with Steve and Anna at 30–50 seconds, then it decreases to 7 seconds after a question. Next after a statement, student talk again rises to 24 seconds, again falls to 14 and 12 in response to questions, and once again recovers to 66 seconds after a statement.

But students do not merely talk more, they talk *differently* when not responding to questions. Their talk has a pronounced flavour of exploration, personal revelation, interpretation of experience, questioning and interconnectedness. More students join in. The students refer to one another's contributions, and combine, elaborate and build upon previous contributions.

At the start, after the teacher has suggested that Paul's and Steve's viewpoints might be two different ways of looking at the same thing, Regina (exchange 1b) goes on to connect Paul's and Steve's views with each other, and then the two with her own: 'I don't see what Paul and Steve said as two separate ideas', she begins. The teacher praises Regina's illustration and Steve comes in with, 'I agree with her almost all the way up until the end, where she said . . .' (exchange 5b). Anna too contributes to the point (exchange 5c).

Towards the end, Chris and Tommy offer contributions and Regina follows at length (exchange 10e). She begins by citing Tommy and Chris to make her own interpretation: 'I think he has a point of view or whatever, but I think, taking from what Chris said, that . . .'. She then incorporates another boy's remarks from four to five exchanges back, to build to her conclusion: 'And just like he said, some parents are . . . So, . . .'.

That is not the kind of talk that follows teacher questions – neither in length nor in quality.

Problematical discussion

A third illustration in yet different circumstances is Mr P's Psychology class (transcript 5). His 27 seniors, almost all of whom are black, have read *The Three Faces of Eve*, and their experienced teacher leads them through an interesting discussion on the problem of multiple personality. He starts by mentioning that they have previously studied the construction of consciousness and today are going to work on the dissociation of consciousness: 'You've read the material. So let's see, ah, summarize that, and then open it up for your observations – or whatever.' The usual sorts of things happen: occasional disorder surfaces, bells ring, and boisterous crowds tramp up and down the stairs just outside the door, going to and from lunch all during this class hour. But some unusual discussion events also occur.

In this episode, we hear about one question per minute – but from *students*. Other odd events follow. Whereas Mr S would ask the occasional question and Mr W would alternate questions and statements, Mr P uses *series* of questions and series of non-question techniques. But the overall effect on discussion is the same: conversational ups and downs, with series of questions that depress student participation alternating with series of non-questions that enhance it. That happens despite the 'good discussion questions' that Mr P asks, including: Suppose X? What then? (exchanges 15, 18, 22) and What would/why not/how come? (exchanges 13, 23).

Student questions appear in the midst of both series, leading to two different results. Three times student questions (exchanges 12b, 22b, 23b) appear in the midst of teacher questions, and participation declines and remains meagre. But when Mr P takes the alternative of *using* student questions, participation surges and discussion gets markedly richer.

When Duane raises a question (exchange 15c), the teacher asks that it be repeated, then he praises it, reiterates and extends it, offering it for discussion. Mitchell (exchange 16c) follows by formulating a corollary question, and the teacher exclaims, 'I don't know' (exchange 17a). Yvonne then gives it an extensive try. Mr P stops her with a question and Yvonne explains, 'I don't know! That's what we're looking for!' (exchange 19b). So the teacher says, 'OK, come on, let's find it!' Whereupon Mike and Darryl (exchange 21b,c) offer two possibilities.

There follows a series of teacher questions and declining participation, including two student questions that come to nothing. But the next four exchanges (25–28) are quite different. The teacher asks no questions. Mr P praises a girl for suggesting something that was not in the book, 'trauma', and Duane (exchange 25b) suggests another possibility. The teacher connects it with 'the trauma model'. Yvonne enters in and the teacher identifies her suggestion as 'the idol model'. Then Mike contributes something which the teacher also praises as not derived from the reading, and which he identifies as 'the conflict model'. Whereupon Anthony suggests yet a fourth possible explanation.

In these last four exchanges the teacher has not used questions but alternatives. In response, four students have proffered, two in a questioning way, different explanations to consider. And each student has spoken at length: Duane for 26 seconds, Yvonne for 37, Mike for 22 and Anthony for 31. Earlier, three possibilities had been offered at length, again in response to non-question interventions: Yvonne (exchange 17b), Mike (exchanges 20b and 21b) and Darryl (exchange 21c).

To characterize the contrast, the students in Mr P's discussion responded twice as long to his non-question alternatives as to his questions (15 *vs* 8 seconds). In addition, the students raised questions, explored possibilities, speculated beyond the reading, and spoke to one another's points. They did not do these things when responding to questions.

Children's discussions

The three cases just reviewed are discussions by older adolescents in American high-schools. Here are three brief cases of discussions by young children in England, Canada and New Zealand, showing us how to foster discussion at exactly the level where discussion is most pressingly needed – right at the start in preschool, kindergarten and first/second grade.

Preschool

In England, Heather and David Wood observed children aged 3–4 years, paired in conversational sessions with a teacher (Wood and Wood 1983). They discovered that the children responded to statements at greater length and initiative than to teacher questions. For instance, their response to the teacher's comments averaged 5.5 words per turn and 69 per cent initiative, compared with 2.7 words and 28 per cent initiative and 3.4 words and 32 per cent initiative for questions of two-choice and wh-types, respectively. Wood and Wood also went on to train teachers of young deaf children aged 6–11, to vary their use of questions and comments during their ten-minute 'News' sessions (Wood and Wood 1984). Again the children spoke at greater length and initiative in response to the statements than to teacher questions: 3.7 words per turn and 83 per cent initiative, compared with 2.5 words and 46 per cent initiative and 1.9 words and 25 per cent initiative for wh- and two-choice questions, respectively. These were experimental variations: when the comments were increased and the questions decreased, participation increased; when questions increased, participation decreased. The same children with the same teacher spoke longer and showed more elaboration, contributions, ideas and questions when the teacher stopped questioning them and substituted instead declarative statements and phatics ('I like going to the park, too'; 'That must have been awful').

Kindergarten

'Show and Tell' is a regular session in kindergarten classrooms during which the children sit clustered about their teacher and talk about their toys, things happening to them, and upcoming events in their lives. To enhance the participation of very shy children, kindergarten teachers in Canada were trained to reduce the number of questions they asked of the children and to increase their statements and phatics (Evans and Bienert 1992). Observation and analysis of the taped sessions revealed that the more the teacher used statements and phatics, and the fewer the number of questions, the greater the participation by shy children in the session. By contrast to sessions with more questions, the children spoke more words and gave more spontaneous contributions – unsolicited comments, questions and contents. In a typical session of twenty exchanges, a shy child would speak on average over ten more words (48 *vs* 37) and over twice as many spontaneous words (21 *vs* 10).

First/second grade

In New Zealand, Dennis Moore and associates (Patrick *et al.* 1992) also trained a teacher to reduce the number of questions she asked during the 'Morning News' sessions with her twenty-one first- and second-graders, and to substitute statements and pauses. Statements included responding to pupil contributions with a declarative statement, or a restatement, or a statement of interest in elaboration ('I'd like to hear more about that'). Pauses were attentive silences for at least three seconds duration when a pupil stopped speaking. On the very first effort, the teacher reduced her questions from 39 to 3 for the ten-minute session, while correspondingly increasing her statements (from 11 to 16) and pauses (from 2 to 6). The effect was to increase child talk to over half the total talk time (from 20 to 33 seconds per minute). When in the next sessions the questions were increased, the children's talk decreased; and when the questions again decreased and the statements and pauses increased, so too did the children's participation increase. 'These results support the hypothesis that teacher questions foil pupil talk in morning news, whereas replacing teacher questions with statements and increasing the use of pauses increases student discourse without adversely affecting classroom behaviour' (ibid.: p. 3).

Discussion in general

In all of these classes, it is as if we see discussion diminishing in the face of teacher questions, resurging when non-questioning alternatives are used – statements, phatics, pauses, student questions – and again receding when the questions resume. Table 5.1 summarizes the results from the case study (Dillon 1985) of the three American high-school discussions and from another study by David and Heather Wood that actually examined these very same three classes (Wood and Wood 1988). Table 5.1 further compares these three discussions (transcripts 3, 4 and 5) with the recitation class conducted by teacher H (transcript 1) – a class which Wood and Wood also studied along with studying the three discussion classes. This unusual and fortunate circumstance of two independent researches into the very same set of classrooms permits us to make a series of contrasts over the effects of using questions and non-question alternatives in discussion classes and, further, in discussion by contrast to recitation classes, while affording yet another contrast between recitation and discussion processes (contrasted over other terms in Chapter 1). Three overall conclusions are evident in Table 5.1.

First, in every case student response was longer to non-question alternatives than to questions. Even in the case of recitation, where 5–6 questions are asked and answered every single minute, constraining student response to a few seconds' burst, the response to alternatives was longer, albeit only one second longer. But in this breathless class, the one second represents a 25 per cent increase over response to questions. In the discussion classes, the response to alternatives was two and three times longer than to questions.

Second, in every case student initiative was greater after alternatives than after questions. To the teacher's comments and phatics students did not just respond at greater length but with more active and energetic dynamics – elaborations, spontaneous contributions, unsolicited material, ideas, and questions of their own. Their overall initiative is apportioned in a way as to significantly discriminate questions and alternatives – the one diminishing initiative, the other enhancing it.

Third, on the one hand discussion distinguishes itself from the question–answer process of recitation by far fewer questions, and on the other by longer student response and greater student initiative, plus far greater student talk overall and many times more student–student exchanges. For instance, the proportion of questions ranges from over three-quarters of the interaction in recitation to one-half and one-quarter in the discussions, while overall student initiative ranges from barely 40 per cent in the recitation to over 60, 80 and 90 per cent in the discussions. And, even within that differential, questions and non-question alternatives in both cases are further finely distinguished by longer responses and greater initiative after alternatives.

Table 5.1 Questioning *vs* alternatives in classroom group talk

			Discussion	
Features of talk	Recitation (H, transcript 1)	Problematical (P, transcript 5)	Informational (S, transcript 3)	Dialectical (W, transcript 4)
Teacher questions				
Overall (%)[a]	76	54	20	26
Rate per minute[b]	5.2	1.8	1.2	0.4
Student response (seconds)[b]				
To questions	4	8	8	15
To alternatives	5	13	13	40
Student initiative (%)[a]				
Overall	39	65	80	93
After questions	30	44	45	100
After alternatives (comments and phatics)	100	100	88	100
Student talk (%)[b]				
Overall	41	64	78	67
Student–student turns	12	39	42	43

[a]From Wood and Wood (1988); [b]from Dillon (1985).

In summary, students responded at greater length to the non-question alternatives than to the questions, and they showed greater initiative. The students did not merely talk more, nor was it mere talk. In response to the alternatives, but not to the questions, their participation exhibited these additional features:

- more student questions;
- more exploration and speculation;
- more reference to personal experience and outside factors;
- more contributed topics and unsolicited material;
- more participants overall and in each exchange;
- more references by students to other students' contributions;
- more student initiative (e.g. spontaneous contributions, ideas).

The alternatives were followed by more student talk and also by more complex thought, deeper personal involvement, wider participation, greater cohesion, stronger dynamics and richer inquiry – in short, by more and better discussion.

These are plainly desirable features of a discussion class. They serve an educative purpose in classroom circumstance, enhancing the students' cognitive, affective and expressive processes. That is how teacher and students should talk in discussion.

6

WHY USE DISCUSSION?

When we search for the rationale of discussion, we find ourselves facing first the many reasons against using discussion and then the reasons for it. Ultimately, we discover the *raison d'être* of discussion. Wherein lies the essential practice of discussion? What considerations above all others urge and even compel us to use discussion? Lastly, we consider some recommendations, wondering what we can do to promote the practice of discussion.

Only its goodness and centrality as an essential educative activity would move us to use discussion, while powerful pragmatic forces frustrate the move and sometimes even the very idea of its attempt. Why, indeed, use discussion?

REASONS AGAINST DISCUSSION

What discourages us from using discussion? All manner of things do. However, only a few of these belong to discussion itself, most notably its difficulty. The major discouragements reflect on the capacities of teachers, principally their indisposition to discuss, and on the conditions of school and social systems, especially their antipathy towards discussion.

Difficulties of discussion

Discussion is difficult. Far from coming naturally, it *has to be learned*. Students as well as teacher have to learn it, the class group as well as individuals; and everyone takes a long time to learn to discuss well together, perhaps several months. Far from being carefree and pleasant, discussion is often *hard to do*. It is hard to participate in – the experience can be arduous and trying, for instance, even when exciting and satisfying; and it is always hard to conduct. Discussion is time-consuming, kaleidoscopically unpredictable in process, and uncertain of outcome as much as unsure of success.

Even for an accomplished ivy-league professor of liberal education in the good old days, telling us about the wonders of discussion (Greene 1954), discussion remains:

> . . . an incredibly difficult pedagogical feat which I, for one, have never in my life pulled off to my entire satisfaction . . . I have never conducted a discussion for which I could honestly credit myself with a grade of more than a 75 out of 100.
>
> (Greene 1954: 36)

I too find it difficult.

Many other drawbacks that are commonly laid to discussion turn out not to be characteristics of discussion itself but complaints that discussion is not something else. People criticize discussion for not covering subject matter content and not conveying a body of information; for not producing results very efficiently; for not being a step-by-step procedure that can be trained, implemented and evaluated using a checklist. These claims actually work as rhetoric discouraging discussion, even though they are identical to criticizing the lecture method for its poor transmission of technicolour images.

Incapacities of teachers

Like most other people but with less reason and to worse effect, teachers generally suffer from an almost poignant *lack of experience* with discussion, along with a helpless *lack of know-how* to lead discussions. Rarely during the course of their own schooling have they participated in good discussions with model teachers and committed classmates. Elsewhere in everyday life they experience other, predominant forms of interaction, but discussion only here and there at best. As a student teacher or candidate, they may not have received instruction, training and practice in leading classroom discussions, and little guidance and sustenance in early attempts at teaching through discussion as a young or probationary teacher.

Above all else, the incapacity of teachers consists of an *indisposition towards discussion* – a basic unwillingness to hold discussions in their class. Teachers typically want to teach well and to see their students learn well. But they do not typically see discussion as part of their scheme of purposes and processes. For one reason or another, they may not wish to discuss the points they are trying to teach, they may not want their class to have a discussion over the matter, and they may not be willing to help the students to discuss and to learn how to discuss – or not now, at any rate; right now the teacher has other things to do and many pressing concerns to meet.

Teachers indisposed towards discussion might not have a strong sentiment of inquiry, interest in student thinking, trust of group processes, nor indeed democratic attitudes generally and in particular towards knowledge and authority. They may be worried about the waste of time in discussion, the not getting anywhere, the curriculum material not being covered, the topic first being opened up and then not being closed down, the immaturity and incorrectness of student opinion, the rise of conflict and emotion in the class, the loss of direction and control over the whole process – all finally leaving them with the debilitating sense that they don't even seem to be *teaching* during discussion. These are powerful reasons against using discussion.

Antipathies of the system

Most powerful of all are systemic conditions in school and society, in which not much discussion can be seen nor much place where it might fit in. School and society are busy promoting other things, and many of these things and the way they are promoted are deadly to discussion.

The predominant features of schooling offer no support to efforts to discuss and moreover actively support its contraries. The structures and processes of schooling, even the physical setting of classrooms – the time, tasks, crowds, furnishings – discourage the use of discussion, along perhaps with many colleagues and administrators, not to mention parents and leaders of business, government and community. Discussion is widely regarded as a waste of time or a needless effort to begin with, pointless in the face of the many urgent tasks that educators are supposed to be getting on with. More darkly, discussion may be sensed as a real threat to the social and linguistic management order of the classroom (Harris 1988).

The antidialogical practices of the school, as listed by Burbules (1993), fall to mournful effect upon discussion. They include curriculum as content coverage, aims as tested outcomes, teaching as management and control, classroom interaction as question–answer recitation; teacher authority and privilege, overcrowded and competitive classrooms. Conditions outside in the antidialogical society are just as forbidding to discussion. Dialogue has become 'an extraordinary and fortuitous exception to the rule', occurring where it does despite dominant social and cultural influences against it (ibid.: p. 150).

Social norms and practices make discussion foreign to our everyday life and experience as well as education. They emphasize individual over group, privacy of thought and pursuit over public participation, and authority and policy instead of community and inquiry as source of knowledge and decision. The dominant pattern of discourse is chatter, assertion, and persuasion if not deception, in contrast to disciplined concert of reason, meaning and deliberation. Efforts to talk about problems in a group situation are invariably countered within moments by a move to get out and at least *do* something, because anything is better than just sitting around and wasting time talking about it. An entire mindset restricts the worth of things to their effectiveness or pay-off in results, products and outcomes, stopping us from entering relations with one another should they look as unproductive as discussion; while an overwhelming lassitude dispenses us from discussion by assigning away our questions and problems for the properly accountable elected or appointed officials to resolve.

In the face of systemic antipathies all around, discussion understandably keeps a low profile.

REASONS FOR DISCUSSION

What encourages us to use discussion? Through discussion things are learned and processes are developed. For instance, we learn the subject matter discussed and we also learn how to discuss – the skills, dispositions and behaviours of discussion. Through discussion growth is also enhanced, our own and our group's, and matters are resolved or made more satisfying. Thus the considerations in favour of discussion count not just products but also processes, and not just intellectual ones but also attitudinal and behavioural ones, and further, not just individual but also communal ones.

Subject matter

We learn the topic being discussed. For instance, we form ideas and sentiments respecting it. We come to know or to understand the subject matter, to appreciate and judge it, to resolve or decide it. At the same time we are also learning to understand, by gaining greater powers of understanding and judging matters.

These things we are likely to learn better through discussion than through most other modes of teaching and learning available in schools. For instance, we are more actively involved in discussion and others are involved with us. We explore the many various facts and perspectives that others bring, and we join them in discovering, developing and scrutinizing new ideas or other proposals on the subject in question.

Discussion processes

We learn how to discuss. That serves the corresponding educational aim of learning how to learn, along with learning the subject matter. Through practising the activity of discussion and being guided, corrected and affirmed in doing it rightly, we develop the skills, attitudes and behaviours of discussion.

For one thing, we develop in *communicative competence*. That includes improving our expressiveness, learning various rules of discourse, and acquiring complex abilities of interaction. We learn to talk better. That is, we learn to express our images in propositional form; to translate our ideas from informal into socially formal language; to organize ideas into coherent expression; to gain speed and fluency of response to an ever changing interactive language situation (Bridges 1979). We learn new forms of discourse. We learn the intellectual, procedural and social rules and conventions governing such things as agendas, transitions, conclusions, how to manage the traffic of talk, how to use personal references, criticism and humour as appropriate to this particular form of group interaction (Bridges 1979).

For another thing, we develop in the *moral culture* of discussion. Discussion initiates us into a special way of acting together, cultivating within us dispositions and virtues of conduct such as those described in Chapter 1 (from Bridges 1979): reasonableness, peaceableness, truthfulness, freedom, equality, respect, responsiveness, judiciousness, reflectiveness, openness.

Personal and group growth

Through discussion we experience personal growth, considered apart from academic learning and communicative competence. For instance, in discussion our personal involvement is deeper, and more significant to us. The dynamics of our self become increasingly active, independent, searching, by contrast to passive, dependent or even infantile, reactive and quiescent. We grow also in interpersonal respects. A review of the literature on adult group discussion (Osinski *et al.* 1972), lists growth in perceptiveness of the feelings and behaviours of others, openness in interrelationships, acceptance of differences in others, understanding and skill as a group member, self-awareness and self-confidence in interaction.

As a corollary, our group too experiences growth through discussion. For instance, group dynamics improve and community or cohesiveness is enhanced. This aspect is beyond our personal and even interpersonal growth. We grow *together*; our *group* experiences growth. Discussion enhances our cognitive, affective and communicative processes and in addition our group's collaborative, constructive and deliberative powers. Above all we learn together those democratic attitudes and behaviours that befit group deliberation in a democratic polity and intellectual inquiry in a free society of thought and action (see Dillon 1994).

Resolution of matters

Not only do we learn things and develop processes through discussion, and not only do benefits accrue to us and to our group: discussion also *does* something to matters considered apart from ourselves as it were. Through discussion matters are resolved, and they are resolved better than by other means (e.g. lecture, authority, voting). For instance, the topic under discussion is illuminated. The question is answered, the problem is solved, the issue is settled – or question, problem, issue is reformulated for more fruitful address.

Not all resolutions are conclusive, forming some final concrete product of discussion. For instance, the question can find reformulation instead of definitive answer. Or the circumstance is clarified. Cooperation forms, resolve strengthens, decisions are pondered and actions promoted. A range of novel alternatives and unsuspected possibilities appear – greater appreciation and awareness, and 'progress in the ascertainment of complexities' (Buchler 1954: 11). Progress can be modest. 'We shall have done well', Lasker (1949: 368) assures us:

> . . . if we have advanced thinking a few steps on some question of common concern, if we have improved our ability to deal practically with tasks beyond the power of the individual, if in searching together for better ways of meeting life's problems, we have advanced a little the cause of human fellowship.

Through discussion matters are resolved, if only making our state of affairs somehow more satisfying.

Efficacy of method

Many other reasons for using discussion have been advanced, claiming particular value regarding the efficacy of discussion as a method of teaching. Here are examples from two perspectives.

Liberal education

From the standpoint of liberal education, Theodore Greene (1954) of Yale University specified five special merits of the discussion method. This method:

- best elicits the total response of the student's personality;
- is most effective in helping students to acquire logical and linguistic proficiency;
- excels in demonstrating the need for the interpretation of evidence – correcting dogmatism and promoting reflective inquiry;
- is the method *par excellence* for practice in responsible evaluation;
- best resists provincialism and promotes synoptic perspectives.

'*In short, the discussion method is, I believe, of unrivalled efficacy in promoting authentic liberal education in the hearts and minds of students*' (Greene 1954: 50). These impressive claims for the efficacy of discussion are made not from research but from the ancient tradition and durable yet fading practice of liberal education, especially in select colleges.

Empirical research

Another set of claims, still bearing on the efficacy of discussion as a method of teaching, has been made from the standpoint of research. For a long time, Mark and Joyce Gall have reviewed studies on the discussion method in teaching (Gall and Gall 1976, 1990). They conclude that research has found the discussion method to be effective for five types of student learning outcomes: general subject matter mastery; problem-solving ability; moral development; attitude change and development; and communication skills. We should recognize that there has not been much research, that is, empirical studies of classroom discussion, and that the available research is neither strong nor clear in supporting the 'effectiveness' of discussion, in the sense of a method of teaching that produces learning outcomes. But that does not matter in the end.

Even if there were no research, we would still use discussion. And we would use it even if an overwhelming body of research demonstrated it either as being effective or wholly ineffective. For we would not use discussion as an instrument or as a technique for the production of outcomes. So the research consideration, the effectiveness consideration and the outcomes consideration are not primary. Neither are the four considerations we have described: learning the subject matter, developing discussion processes, personal and group growth, resolution of matters.

These are important reasons, to be sure. They are persuasive considerations that encourage us to use discussion. But none of these considerations is in the end primary or ultimate. There is something else about discussion that, even more than these factors, and apart from them, encourages us to use discussion and actually urges and compels us to discuss – as if discussion were an activity good in and of itself. That would constitute the be-all and end-all of discussion, its *raison d'être*. What would that be?

RAISON D'ÊTRE OF DISCUSSION

We engage in discussion for the very practice of essential goods. We discuss for the experience of community and inquiry in the lived moment, for participation with our fellows in communal reflection, discovery and deliberation. Discussion is a good way for us to be together. We use it to face our common perplexities about what to think and how to act. And we use it to form our young, inducing them into these very goods. So discussion is a way for adults and children to be together in a fundamental human relation and essential educative activity. That is the good of discussion, its *raison d'être*.

This perspective on discussion is difficult to communicate. It is a strange way of viewing things in this modern world, where things are overwhelmingly regarded as good not in themselves but for the things that they produce – the money they make, the results they get, the goals and targets they achieve, their products and outcomes, their efficiency, instrumentality, utility, and so forth. On that modern, technical-production view, we are presumed to find the justification and worth of discussion in the learning that it produces in students, especially by contrast to other approaches. We are presumed to regard discussion as a technique competing with others in the gimmickry of efficient production of outcomes. That, however, is not the essence of discussion, but only its character under duress, as it were, when put to use as an instrument – when, given preset goals and objectives, discussion is wielded, as one among other means and tools, to see how productively it achieves these external ends.

Now, the various learnings that students might experience through discussion are helpful and important considerations in favour of discussion, but they are not of the essence of discussion, nor are they compelling reasons for using discussion in classrooms and other educational settings. It is not that these learnings are to be dismissed or undervalued. They are in fact good things, worthy and precious some of them, and we are glad when through discussion our children learn subject matters, learn how to discuss, learn democratic attitudes and behaviours, and so on. But they are not the *raison d'être* of discussion. The worth of discussion is not given by the worth of these learnings, but by other goods intrinsic to itself.

Within discussion are found the goods that make it a fundamental and essential educative activity – apart from other goods that may accrue. Discussion is 'educationally ultimate' says Paterson (1970: 44–5):

> I for one should certainly wish to claim that the members of an adult class, exploring in common the meaning of some subject by engaging in a completely open activity of free mutual address, are engaged in an activity which requires no further justification, even if their assimilation of the material under study, their grasp of its principles, and their mastery of the relevant skills are not in the slightest augmented as a result of their discussion . . . Discussion is rather the educational activity *par excellence*,

an educational end-in-itself, and to participate in discussion is to share in one of the educational ultimates to
which the accumulation of factual knowledge, the use of
teaching aids, and the practice of educational techniques
are nothing but the useful and necessary preliminaries.

Such a view clearly does not proceed from the modern
paradigm of teaching as a technical-production function. But
post-modern critical theory has recovered this traditional view.
From that perspective, Nicholas Burbules (1993) in his book,
Dialogue in Teaching, stresses from start to finish that dialogue is a
relation that we enter into. We are drawn to enter it for its
animating spirit of equality, mutuality and cooperation, as an
arena where we and others are bound in relations of mutual
appreciation, challenge and stimulation (ibid.: pp. 65, 143). We do
not use discussion for something else but we enter into it for the
goods that are within the doing of the very activity itself.

The worth of discussion is not to be sought in events
subsequent to and external to itself but found within the very
process of discussion. Among these goods are the encompassing
entailments of mutuality and concert as we live, think and act in
communal circumstance. That is the way for educators and
students to live and work together in classroom circumstances as
they wonder what to think and how to act about the topics they
are engaging over.

That is an ancient usage of discussion, durable until now but
disappearing from our schools. It is the practice exemplified by
Socrates and others from his day and ours who inspire us to find
out together through discussion what is right and true and then to
act it, all the while reflecting and deliberating together about the
goodness of our thought and action. What can we do to promote
this practice of discussion?

RECOMMENDATIONS

Researchers might *describe the good use of discussion*. Rather than
demonstrate or vindicate discussion by its outcomes or effectiveness by contrast to other methods, studies might describe in

helpful detail the ongoing processes of discussion and the conditions of its use and success in classrooms. We need to know just what discussion looks like when it is going well in a classroom, and what we and our school might need to give discussion a better chance. We urgently need to know about discussion, especially in kindergarten and the first and second years of school. We need, too, a rhetorical service from thoughtful scholars who will write to exhort and to move us to action, who will acclaim the right use of discussion and cheer us on in its practice. These descriptions and exhortations should appear in magazines and journals for teachers and administrators, in pamphlets, bulletins, newsletters and informally published materials that practitioners might see as they go about their daily work.

For willing teachers, the one recommendation is to *practise discussion*. Willing administrators and other educators might help teachers to initiate and to sustain the practice. We urgently need to arouse discussion, especially in kindergarten and the first and second years of school. Willing though we are, we might still feel that we don't know that much about discussion and aren't quite sure of how to go about it. Through study and observation and through participation and reflection, we can learn about discussion for ourselves. But we also need to start *doing* it with our children, now, and thereafter to *keep on* doing it. It is a matter of long and faithful trying. We persevere with our practice as we slowly come to use discussion rightly in our circumstance, inducing our young into the educative goods nowhere else available to them and through them to all the rest of us.

REFERENCES

Alvermann, D. and Hayes, D. (1989). Classroom discussion of content reading assignments: An intervention study. *Reading Research Quarterly*, **24**, 305–335.

Alvermann, D., O'Brien, D. and Dillon, D. (1990). What teachers do when they say they're having discussions of content area reading assignments. *Reading Research Quarterly*, **25**, 296–322.

Barnlund, D. and Haiman, F. (1960). *The dynamics of discussion*. Boston, MA: Houghton Mifflin.

Barrett-Lennard, G. (1962). *Teacher–Pupil Relationship Inventory: Pupil Form*. Adaptation of Therapist–Client Relationship Inventory. *Psychological Monographs*, **76**, 43 (Whole No. 562).

Bernier, R. (1993). What is the character of discussion in the kindergarten classroom and what conditions invite or discourage its use? Seminar paper for Education 245I, Spring 1993, School of Education, University of California, Riverside.

Bridges, D. (1979). *Education, democracy and discussion*. Windsor: NFER. Reprinted 1988 by University Press of America.

Bridges, D. (1988). A philosophical analysis of discussion. In J.T. Dillon (Ed.), *Questioning and discussion: A multidisciplinary study*, pp. 15–28. Norwood, NJ: Ablex.

Bridges, D. (1990). The character of discussion: A focus on students. In W. Wilen (Ed.), *Teaching and learning through discussion*, pp. 97–112. Springfield, IL: Thomas.

Buchler, J. (1954). What is a discussion? *Journal of General Education*, **8**, 7–17.

Burbules, N. (1993). *Dialogue in teaching: Theory and practice.* New York: Teachers College.

Conner, J. and Chalmers-Neubauer, I. (1989). Mrs. Schuster adopts discussion. *English Education*, **21**, 30–8.

Dillon, J.T. (1985). Using questions to foil discussion. *Teaching and Teacher Education*, **1**, 109–21.

Dillon, J.T. (1988a). *Questioning and teaching: A manual of practice.* London: Routledge/New York: Teachers College.

Dillon, J.T. (Ed.) (1988b). *Questioning and discussion: A multidisciplinary study.* Norwood, NJ: Ablex.

Dillon, J.T. (1988c). Discussion vs. recitation. *Tennessee Educational Leadership*, **15**, 52–64.

Dillon, J.T. (1990). *The practice of questioning.* London: Routledge.

Dillon, J.T. (1994). The questions of deliberation. In J.T. Dillon (Ed.), *Deliberation in education and society.* Norwood, NJ: Ablex.

Dreyfus, A. and Lieberman, R. (1981). Perceptions, expectations and interactions: The essential ingredients for a genuine classroom discussion. *Journal of Biological Education*, **15**, 153–7.

Evans, M. and Bienert, H. (1992). Control and paradox in teacher conversations with shy children. *Canadian Journal of Behavioral Science*, **24**, 502–16.

Fasching, J. and Erickson, B. (1985). Group discussions in the chemistry classroom and the problem-solving skills of students. *Journal of Chemical Education*, **62**, 842–6.

Francis, E. (1986). *Learning to discuss.* Edinburgh: Moray House College.

Francis, E. (1988). Group processes. In J.T. Dillon (Ed.), *Questioning and discussion: A multidisciplinary study*, pp. 259–79. Norwood, NJ: Ablex.

Francis, E. and Davidson, J. (1986). *Working together on discussion.* Edinburgh: Moray House College.

Gall, J. and Gall, M. (1990). Outcomes of the discussion method. In W. Wilen (Ed.), *Teaching and learning through discussion: The theory, research, and practice of the discussion method*, pp. 25–44. Springfield, IL: Thomas.

Gall, M. and Gall, J. (1976). The discussion method. In N. Gage (Ed.), *The psychology of teaching methods*, pp. 166–216. Chicago, IL: National Society for the Study of Education.

Goodlad, J. (1984). *A place called school.* New York: McGraw-Hill.

Great Books Foundation (1991). *An introduction to shared inquiry*, 2nd ed. Chicago, IL: The Great Books Foundation.

Greene, T. (1954). The art of responsible conversation. *Journal of General Education*, **8**, 34–50.

Haroutunian-Gordon, S. (1991). *Turning the soul: Teaching through conversation in the high school*. Chicago, IL: University of Chicago Press.

Harris, J. (1988). Discussion in practice: Theorising structure and subjectivity in teaching and learning. *British Journal of Sociology of Education*, **9**, 205–21.

Hendrix, J., Mertens, T. and Smith, J. (1983). Facilitating effective small group discussions of controversial issues. *Journal of College Science Teaching*, **13**, 21–5.

Hoyles, C. (1985). What is the point of group discussion in mathematics? *Educational Studies in Mathematics*, **16**, 205–14.

Jersild, A. (1955). *When teachers face themselves*. New York: Teachers College.

Johnson, M. (1979). *Discussion dynamics*. Rowley, MA: Newbury.

Klinzing, H.G. and Floden, R. (1990). Learning to moderate discussions. In W. Wilen (Ed.), *Teaching and learning through discussion*, pp. 175–202. Springfield, IL: Thomas.

Lasker, B. (1949). *Democracy through discussion*. New York: Wilson.

McBurney, J. and Hance, K. (1950). *Discussion in human affairs*. New York: Harper.

McComb, K. and Jablin, F. (1984). Verbal correlates of interviewer empathic listening and employment interview outcomes. *Communication Monographs*, **51**, 353–71.

Maier, N. (1963). *Problem-solving discussions and conferences: Leadership methods and skills*. New York: McGraw-Hill.

Mills, T. (1964). *Group transformation: An analysis of a learning group*. Englewood Cliffs, NJ: Prentice-Hall.

Mishler, E. (1978). Studies in dialogue and discourse: III. Utterance structure and utterance function in interrogative sequences. *Journal of Psycholinguistic Research*, **7**, 279–305.

Moos, R. and Humphrey, B. (1974). *Group Environment Scale: Form R*. Palo Alto, CA: Consulting Psychologists Press.

Osinski, F., Ohliger, J. and McCarthy, C. (1972). *Toward Gog and Magog or?: A critical review of the literature of adult group discussion*. Syracuse, NY: Syracuse University.

Paterson, R. (1970). The concept of discussion: A philosophical approach. *Studies in Adult Education*, **2**, 28–50.

Patrick, H., Orsborne, E., Dixon, R. and Moore, D. (1992). The effects of reducing teacher questions and increasing pauses on child talk during morning news. Education Department, University of Auckland, New Zealand.

Phillips, G., Pedersen, D. and Wood, J. (1979). *Group discussion: A practical guide to participation and leadership*. Boston, MA: Houghton Mifflin.

Roby, T. (1988). Models of discussion. In J.T. Dillon (Ed.), *Questioning and discussion: A multidisciplinary study*, pp. 163–91. Norwood, NJ: Ablex.

Rowe, M.B. (1974). Pausing phenomena: Influence on the quality of instruction. *Journal of Psycholinguistic Research*, 3, 203–233.

Rudduck, J. (1978). *Learning through small group discussion*. Guildford: Society for Research into Higher Education, University of Surrey.

St John's College (1993). *Catalog*. Annapolis, MD and Sante Fe, NM.

Salzberger-Wittenberg, I., Henry, G. and Osborne, E. (1983). *The emotional experience of learning and teaching*. London: Routledge and Kegan Paul.

Sattler, W. and Miller, N. (1954). *Discussion and conference*. New York: Prentice-Hall.

Scheidel, T. and Crowell, L. (1979). *Discussing and deciding: A desk book for group leaders and members*. New York: Macmillan.

Stodolsky, S., Ferguson, T. and Wimpelberg, K. (1981). The recitation persists, but what does it look like? *Journal of Curriculum Studies*, 13, 121–30.

Swift, N. and Gooding, C. (1983). Interaction of wait time feedback and questioning instruction on middle school science teaching. *Journal of Research in Science Teaching*, 20, 721–30.

Thelen, H. (1954). *Dynamics of groups at work*. Chicago, IL: University of Chicago Press.

Tobin, K. (1987). The role of wait time in higher cognitive level learning. *Review of Educational Research*, 57, 69–95.

VanMents, M. (1990). *Active talk: The effective use of discussion in learning*. London: Kegan Page/New York: St Martin.

Wood, D. and Wood, H. (1988). Questioning versus student initiative. In J.T. Dillon (Ed.), *Questioning and discussion: A multidisciplinary study*, pp. 280–305. Norwood, NJ: Ablex.

Wood, H. and Wood, D. (1983). Questioning the pre-school child. *Educational Review*, 35, 149–62.

Wood, H. and Wood, D. (1984). An experimental evaluation of the effects of five styles of teacher conversation on the language of hearing-impaired children. *Journal of Child Psychology and Psychiatry*, 25, 45–62.

BIBLIOGRAPHY ON DISCUSSION

This classified and annotated bibliography offers a select guide for further study of discussion in its various respects and through various resources: general treatments of the concept and pedagogy of discussion; anthologies of studies on discussion; studies on discussion in the subject matters of maths, sciences, social studies and language arts; source materials of literature reviews and bibliographies on discussion; and textbooks on discussion in general, including in society.

Only selected sources are listed here. The entries are selected from works that are (a) published, (b) in English, (c) during the last two decades or so, and (d) relating to discussion in the field of education. Although three dozen of the five dozen items are from the 1980s and 1990s, two dozen texts dating from the 1940s and 1950s are also included for reference to the older and better literature on discussion generally. Finally, this listing excludes works that do not bear on discussion specifically as a particular kind of group talk, rather than any sort of verbal exchange. Thus, for example, the excellent book *Discussion Dynamics* is excluded despite its title, because it describes the dynamics of classroom recitation, not discussion.

I GENERAL TREATMENTS

Concept of discussion

Bridges, D. (1979). *Education, democracy and discussion.* Windsor: NFER. Reprinted 1988 by University Press of America.

Greene, T. (1954). The art of responsible conversation. *Journal of General Education,* **8,** 34–50.

Harris, J. (1988). Discussion in practice: Theorizing structure and subjectivity in teaching and learning. *British Journal of Sociology of Education,* **9,** 205–21.

Paterson, R. (1970). The concept of discussion: A philosophical approach. *Studies in Adult Education,* **2,** 28–50.

Sattler, W. (1943). Socratic dialectic and modern group discussion. *Quarterly Journal of Speech,* **29,** 152–7.

Pedagogy of discussion

Armstrong, M. and Boud, D. (1983). Assessing participation in discussion: An exploration of the issues. *Studies in Higher Education,* **8,** 33–44.

Dillon, J.T. (1988). *Questioning and teaching: A manual of practice.* London: Routledge/New York: Teachers College. Chapters on using student and teacher questions, and alternatives, in discussion.

Francis, E. (1986). *Learning to discuss.* Edinburgh: Moray House College.

Great Books Foundation (1991). *An introduction to shared inquiry,* 2nd edn. Chicago, IL: Great Books Foundation.

Mills, T. (1964). *Group transformation: An analysis of a learning group.* Englewood Cliffs, NJ: Prentice-Hall.

Rudduck, J. (1978). *Learning through small group discussion: A study of seminar work in higher education.* Guildford: Society for Research into Higher Education, University of Surrey.

Thelen, H. (1954). *Dynamics of groups at work.* Chicago, IL: University of Chicago.

Welty, W. (1989). Discussion method teaching. *Change,* **21**(4), 40–9.

II ANTHOLOGIES

Dillon, J.T. (Ed.) (1988). *Questioning and discussion: A multidisciplinary study.* Norwood, NJ: Ablex. Studies of the same set of discussions from perspectives of philosophy (Bridges), sociolinguistics (Farrar), social psychology (Mullen), logic (Macmillan), cognitive-developmental psychology (Siegel) and organizational psychology (Lighthall); and studies on models of discussion (Roby), wait-time (Swift and Gooding), questions and responses (Klinzing), questions and arguments (Russell), group processes (Francis), questioning versus student initiative (Wood); includes five transcripts of high-school discussions.

Dillon, J.T. (Ed.) (1994). *Deliberation in education and society.* Norwood, NJ: Ablex. Chapters on the concepts and principles of group deliberation in general (Dillon), for curriculum (Reid) and schooling (Westbury), decision-making (Bridges), and the management of complexity (Genelot); and chapters on cases and methods of deliberation in colleges (Atkins), curriculum conferences (Mulder) and schools (Holt), with guidelines (Noyé) and precepts (Brann) for deliberating; includes a bibliography on deliberation in general, in education and in society.

Hayes, A. (Ed.) (1954). The discussion method of teaching: A symposium. *Journal of General Education,* **8,** 2–71. A special journal issue with articles on college discussion (Buchler), liberal education (Wegener), lecture and discussion (Loud), responsible conversation (Greene), and eros and education (Schwab).

Wilen, W. (Ed.) (1990). *Teaching and learning through discussion: The theory, research, and practice of the discussion method.* Springfield, IL: Thomas. Chapters on the forms and phases of discussion (Wilen), outcomes of discussion (Gall), teacher behaviours (Costa), non-question alternatives (Dillon), student understanding (Bridges), teacher social power (Kindsvatter), strategic discussion (Hyman), different social and cultural groups (White) and learning to moderate discussions (Klinzing and Floden).

III STUDIES IN VARIOUS SUBJECT MATTERS

Mathematics

Dahlke, R. and Morash, R. (1982). Discussion in college math. *Improving College and University Teaching,* **30,** 56–60.

Hoyles, C. (1985). What is the point of group discussion in mathematics? *Educational Studies in Mathematics,* **16,** 205–14.

Sciences

Dreyfus, A. and Lieberman, R. (1981). Perceptions, expectations and interactions: The essential ingredients for a genuine classroom discussion. *Journal of Biological Education,* **15,** 153–7.

Fasching, J. and Erickson, B. (1985). Group discussions in the chemistry classroom and the problem-solving skills of students. *Journal of Chemical Education,* **62,** 842–6.

Goodenough, D. (1991). Changing ground: A medical school lecturer turns to discussion teaching. In C. Christensen, D. Garvin and A. Sweet (Eds), *Education for judgment: The artistry of discussion leadership,* pp. 83–98. Boston, MA: Harvard Business School Press.

Hendrix, J., Mertens, T. and Smith, J. (1983). Facilitating effective small group discussions of controversial issues. *Journal of College Science Teaching,* **13,** 21–5.

Karr, M., Barber, K., Van Scoyoc, G., Ahlrichs, J. and McFee, W. (1988). Three-phase discussion sessions. *Journal of Agronomic Education,* **17,** 77–80.

Social studies

Dillon, J.T. (1981). Discussion characteristics in a sample of religion and social studies classes. *Character Potential: A Record of Research,* **9,** 203–5.

Dillon, J.T. (1985). Using questions to foil discussion. *Teaching and Teacher Education,* **1,** 109–21.

Hahn, C. and Avery, P. (1985). Effect of value analysis discussions on students' political attitudes and reading comprehension. *Theory and Research in Social Education,* **13,** 47–60.

Hansen, W. (1983). Improving classroom discussion in economic courses. *Journal of Economic Education,* **14,** 40–9.

Kelly, T. (1989). Leading class discussions of controversial issues. *Social Education,* **53,** 368–70.

Madar, D. (1982). Using nominal group technique to foster productive behaviour in group discussions. *Teaching Political Science,* **9,** 185–9.

Language arts

Alpert, B. (1987). Active, silent and controlled discussions: Explaining variations in classroom conversation. *Teaching and Teacher Education,* **3,** 29–40.

Alvermann, D. and Hayes, D. (1989). Classroom discussion of content area reading assignments: An intervention study. *Reading Research Quarterly*, **24**, 305–35.

Alvermann, D., O'Brien, D. and Dillon, D. (1990). What teachers do when they say they're having discussions of content area reading assignments: A qualitative analysis. *Reading Research Quarterly*, **25**, 296–322.

Conner, J. and Chalmers-Neubauer, I. (1989). Mrs. Schuster adopts discussion: A four-week experiment in an English classroom. *English Education*, **21**, 30–8.

Haroutunian-Gordon, S. (1991). *Turning the soul: Teaching through conversation in the high school*. Chicago, IL: University of Chicago Press (literature).

Yelon, S. and Cooper. C. (1984). Discussion: A naturalistic study of a teaching method. *Instructional Science*, **13**, 213–24 (writing).

IV SOURCE MATERIALS

Reviews

Dillon, J.T. (1984). Research on questioning and discussion. *Educational Leadership*, **42**(3), 50–6.

Dillon, J.T. (1990). *The practice of questioning*. London: Routledge. Chapter 13, 'Research on questions vs. alternatives', pp. 208–36.

Dillon, J.T. (1994). Discussion. *International Encyclopedia of Education*, 2nd edn. Oxford: Elsevier Science Limited.

Gall, J. and Gall, M. (1990). Outcomes of the discussion method. In W. Wilen (Ed.), *Teaching and learning through discussion*, pp. 25–44. Springfield, IL: Thomas.

Gall, M. and Gall, J. (1976). The discussion method. In N. Gage (Ed.), *The psychology of teaching methods*, pp. 166–216. Chicago, IL: National Society for the Study of Education.

Osinski, F., Ohlinger, J. and McCarthy, C. (1972). *Toward Gog and Magog or?: A critical review of the literature of adult group discussion*. Syracuse, NY: Syracuse University.

Bibliographies

Dillon, J.T. (Ed.) (1994). *Deliberation in education and society*. Norwood, NJ: Ablex. 'Bibliography on deliberation', pp. 259–61, with 40 items on deliberation in general, in education and in society.

McBurney, J. and Hance, K. (1950). *Discussion in human affairs*. New York: Harper. (Original edition, *The principles and methods of discussion*, 1939). 'Bibliography', pp. 408–19, with 170 items 'directly on discussion'.

Osinski, F., Ohliger, J. and McCarthy, C. (1972). *Toward Gog and Magog or?: A critical review of the literature of adult group discussion*. Syracuse, NY: Syracuse University. 'Bibliography', pp. 61–80, with 180 items, mostly from the 1960s, and not all on discussion specifically.

Sattler, W. and Miller, N. (1954). *Discussion and conference*. New York: Prentice-Hall. 'Selected bibliography', pp. 311–18, with 130 items, and with articles sub-classified by purposes and types of discussion, leadership, participation and problem solving.

V TEXTBOOKS

Barnlund, D. and Haiman, F. (1960). *The dynamics of discussion*. Boston, MA: Houghton Mifflin.

Ewbank, H. and Auer, J. (1951). *Discussion and debate: Tools of a democracy*, 2nd edn. New York: Appleton-Century-Crofts (1st edn, 1941).

Gulley, H. (1968). *Discussion, conference, and group process*, 2nd edn. New York: Holt, Rinehart and Winston.

Howell, W. and Smith, D. (1956). *Discussion*. New York: Macmillan.

Lasker, B. (1949). *Democracy through discussion*. New York: Wilson.

McBurney, J. and Hance, K. (1950). *Discussion in human affairs*. New York: Harper (1st edn, *The principles and methods of discussion*, 1939).

Maier, N. (1963). *Problem-solving discussions and conferences: Leadership methods and skills*. New York: McGraw-Hill.

Phillips, G., Pedersen, D. and Wood, J. (1979). *Group discussion: A practical guide to participation and leadership*. Boston, MA: Houghton Mifflin.

Sattler, W. and Miller, N. (1954). *Discussion and conference*. New York: Prentice-Hall.

Scheidel, T. and Crowell, L. (1979). *Discussing and deciding: A desk book for group leaders and members*. New York: Macmillan.

PRACTICAL EXERCISES

1 *Formulating the discussion question*

Identify a useful question for a proposed discussion of some subject matter that you are studying – a topic from this book, for example, or a lecture heard in another course, or another book you are reading or movie you have seen. The idea is to take some unit of subject matter that you are involved with (not necessarily as a teacher) and practise formulating a good discussion question for it. If you are a student in a course, you and other students might each formulate the discussion question that you would pose if conducting a discussion on a given chapter or topic from this book, or other readings and topics in your course. Then you can all meet and discuss the merits of the different questions as candidates for the discussion question.

2 *Making a question outline*

For some discussion question or other major issue in school or society, practise outlining the matter in terms of questions. Sketch out several possible answers for each sub-question, or at least for the main question. If you are outlining a known subject such as a book or lecture, identify the answer that it gives to each of the questions. Then note the questions that you might raise and discuss these question–answer propositions. Compare your question outlines with those of other students doing this exercise on the same subject matter. Apart from a course, the next time you find yourself having to think through some matter or to outline any matter at all, try outlining it in questions.

3 *Conducting a practice discussion*

Taking advantage of previous exercises, if you have done them, move ahead and conduct a 10–20 minute discussion on a selected topic from this or another book in the course, using the discussion question and outline from exercises 1 and 2. With the concurrence of your course instructor or programme director, invite five or so agreeable colleagues to serve as participants in the discussion conducted by you as teacher or leader. Another possibility is for several students each to conduct a discussion with different groups of fellow students as participants, while the rest of the class observes the practice discussion and later offers helpful comments. That session might naturally evolve into a genuine discussion of how to conduct a discussion, with the added benefit that everyone will be talking about the same case or cases in common just experienced together (see 11 below for a related exercise).

4 *Conversing without questions*

The next time that you are introduced to a child or meet up with one in some social situation, start speaking to him or her by making some declarative statement, and continue to avoid asking any questions at all for at least your next five turns at talk. Notice how you and other adults tend to talk to children in questions, and how hard it is not to ask them questions and yet still keep talking with them. After some practice with this exercise, observe the results on the child's talk. Ponder your tendency to ask questions during class discussion, and wonder about the beneficial effects of not asking questions but using non-question alternatives instead.

5 *Restating a contribution*

You can do this exercise in a social situation or you can try it for a moment or two as you teach your class. After some child has made a contribution to the ongoing talk, give the child your best understanding of what he or she has just said and also meant, restating it in an economical and accurate sentence, with just the right emphasis and tone to it. Observe the result on the child's talk. You might tape-record some part of your class and then, stopping the tape after a student contribution, voice aloud a practice 'reflective restatement'. Vary the exercise by practising other types of statements and other non-question alternatives in response to the ongoing contributions you hear on the tape.

6 *Maintaining silence*

At two different points in a conversation or in your classroom talk, try maintaining silence for a count of five just after the other person has ostensibly finished speaking. Keep looking gently at the speaker or other participants, and nod and sing 'Baa, baa, black sheep' (as explained in Chapter 5), or otherwise maintain attentive, appreciative, deliberate silence. Note what happens next to the process of talk. Perhaps keep on with this exercise once or twice a day until you and the students get better practised with this odd teacher behaviour. Then you can start applying it consistently at many points during a class discussion.

7 *Summarizing the class' state of mind*

At any major point during a class that you are participating in – at a transition, or a break, for example – try whispering to yourself or jotting down two or three sentences that capture the class' present status in relation to the subject matter. If you are teaching in a class, try this exercise aloud once or twice during a day, not necessarily during a discussion period but during any sort of class activity. Also compose a summary at the end of the teaching day, or as you prepare for the next day. As time goes by, practise helping your students to make summaries, and compare their summaries with yours.

8 *Identifying the question remaining*

You might do this exercise in conjunction with the one on summarizing (exercise 7). As a student, identify the question that remains when the class has completed a given activity or reached some similar point such as a transition or pause. Ask yourself: What question is still left hanging? What question, or aspects of the question, did we not consider about this subject matter? Or ask yourself: Now that we have settled that question, what is the next question to consider? Meet with another student and compare the different questions that you have identified. As a teacher, do this exercise aloud in class. You might practise helping the students, too, to identify the questions that remain. As a reader or other observer, try to keep alert to the questions that the author or speaker is not treating but ought to and/or the question that remains in your mind after pondering the author's treatment.

9 *Observing a discussion*

Arrange to visit a class during a period when the teacher is planning to hold a discussion. Come well prepared to observe the discussion in a methodical way. For instance, decide just what you are going to look at, for what purpose, and in which specific way. Watch the students, in particular. Afterwards, talk with the teacher and pupils, if possible, to discover their purposes and perceptions of the session, so that you will better understand the points that you both missed and managed to observe. Offer to tell the teacher what you have seen and understood about the discussion.

10 *Observing a non-discussion*

Do exercise 9 on a non-discussion, for instance a class recitation, a TV talk show, a political debate or a social conversation. Systematically apply the principles of discussion to the observed talk, coming to appreciate by contrast what discussion is.

11 *Conducting a brief discussion*

Instead of attempting an hour-long discussion, try starting with just a few minutes of it. You can try discussion at the start of an activity and also in the midst of an activity when an interesting issue arises. It might be enough for the class to voice and respond to three or four viewpoints on the matter that you will have first identified and will now summarize. If you have children at home, you might first engage in short discussions with your children, in order to realize and exercise the dispositions and sentiments informing discussion, such as your sincere interest in hearing what the child thinks about the matter under discussion. Practise at home and in school whenever the chance arises, for a few exchanges here and there, then for longer planned periods. Keep on practising.

Further exercises for Chapter 1

12 Select and act out any one of the moral dispositions and other qualities of discussion.
13 Find out from students and teacher their perceptions of a class discussion that you observed, or find these out from your own class.
14 Apply the principles of discussion to contrast a recitation and a discussion, and to analyse your own discussion.

Further exercises for Chapter 2

15 Present to specialists in other subject matters the list of considerations in favour of discussion in physics.

16 Reformulate in terms more conducive to discussion the defective
questions listed in this chapter, or other questions in other classes or
on the radio and TV.

17 Work out the various aspects of your given subject matter that
students might discuss.

Further exercises for Chapter 3

18 Try any of five different ways of learning about discussion.

19 Identify one or two important questions that you personally are not
willing to discuss.

20 Provide yourself with some experience in group dynamics while also
reading something about it, and reflect on that experience and
reading in terms helpful to class discussion.

Further exercises for Chapter 4

21 Try any of five ways of preparing for discussion as a student.

22 Prepare and rehearse the physical presentation of a discussion
question.

23 Try any of five leadership functions in the next discussion you join
in.

24 Reconstruct the question outline of this book.

25 Identify misbehaviours in some actual class discussion.

Further exercises for Chapter 5

26 Recollect the questions you have asked over the past few days, and
cull out the ones that genuinely perplexed you.

27 The next time a child or student raises a question, act to sustain the
asking rather than answer the question.

28 Try any of a dozen alternatives to questioning during a class or social
conversation.

Further exercises for Chapter 6

29 Identify and act to overcome one small barrier to your use of
discussion in your classroom.

30 Start practising discussion the next time you teach a class. Keep on
practising discussion.

CLASSROOM
TRANSCRIPTS

1 H's history recitation

H: OK, so we've kind of covered leadership and some of the things that Washington brought with it. Why else did they win? Leadership is important, that's one.

S: France gave 'em help.

H: OK, so France giving aid is an example of what? France is an example of it, obviously.

S: Aid from allies.

H: Aid from allies, very good. Were there any other allies who gave aid to us?

S: Spain.

H: Spain. Now, when you say aid, can you define that?

S: Help.

H: Define 'help'. Spell it out for me.

S: Assistance.

H: Spell it out for me.

S: They taught the men how to fight the right way.

H: Who taught?

S: The allies.

H: Where? When?

S: In the battlefield.

H: In the battlefield?

  . . . and so on.

2 T's history discussion

T: The treatment that Louis XIV gave to the Huguenots is anything but acceptable, and yet some people say that he was justified in his treatment of the Huguenots, in respect to the point that he was trying to take care of his country. Do you feel that Louis was justified in his treatment of the Huguenots? – Rosa.

Rosa: I think, you know, they had their religion and stuff like that. I don't think he should have gone as far as totally kicking them out of the country and giving them, like, social disgrace, you know, like taking their jobs away from them. If they wouldn't interfere with his way of ruling, and their religion, why should he interfere with them?   [T: Ken.]

Ken: He's partially right in what he did, but I don't feel he should've kicked them out, like she said. 'Cause who is he to say how they can [—], you know? Even though it's all Catholics, he gave 'em, like, religious freedom.   [T: Barb.]

Barb: I feel, I feel that he had hardly any justification at all. He wound up at the end, as Lydia said, having to almost be persuaded by all the people around him that were saying, 'Well, look at the Huguenots'. You know, 'Why don't you do something about the Huguenots? We don't like the Huguenots' . . . [continues] . . . It was one of the last places that he had to conquer, so he figured he'd just go out and then kill 'em. I think it was totally unfair.

T: OK, I can see where you're coming from, but I don't know if I can totally agree with that. Is there anyone who disagrees with what these people are saying? – Marty.

Marty: I don't really disagree, but you know, we know the story, how everything worked out . . . [continues] . . . They wanted to get rid of the Huguenots. And just like that, you know, us here, we don't like somebody, like, you know, Italians and Nazis – sorta the same thing, something like that, in their eyes. I don't think he was justified himself.   [T: Diane.]

Diane: OK, in those days the church and state were like the same thing and everything, and so I think, well, like Louis – well, it isn't like today, when you can be a member of a country, just a member of a country. In those days, the church and the country meant the same thing, and when he saw people breaking away from the church, then he thought that they were breaking away from him. And he wanted to stop it. That was about the only thing he could do.

T: So you feel that he was justified in what he was doing, as far as he was concerned – he could justify it to himself.

Diane: Yeah, he could justify it to himself. But then, before then they really didn't have a separation. So all he could see was an allegory. And he wanted to pull back on that.

T: All right, Marty raised an interesting point just a few seconds ago. He said that . . . [continues about Communists and Nazis in Chicago] . . . It's getting away from France, but again it's speaking about the same idea – acceptance of groups that are going against the norms of your society. What's your opinion on groups of this type? Should they be allowed, should they be censored, should it be washed over, should there be guidelines, stipulations – should there be control like Louis XIV tried to control them, to be done away with? – Julie.

Julie: I think that they should be allowed to speak their opinion, because . . . [continues] . . . But they should be allowed to speak their opinion, you don't have to listen.   [T: OK, Sean.]

Sean: I think Marty was wrong, because . . . [continues] . . . Look what they did like, back I think in the 50s with the Communists, and McCarthy, and then during World War II with the Japanese. So, it's still going on today.

T: Right, and the concentration camps which we have had inside the United States during World War II, to house Japanese-Americans because you couldn't trust the Japanese. All right, so he's totally disagreeing with what you had to say, Marty.

Marty: Yeah, well . . . No, he brought up a good point . . . [continues] . . . But I mean, I don't think Thomas Jefferson and those guys who signed the Constitution would like Nazis around here. Especially after what they did. I think that's why –

George: – They come over here from another country for three months and they earn an ADC [welfare] check! My parents have been working for 25 some odd years, and they're not getting half the money that [ethnic epithet] are getting nowadays.

T: Yes, we know . . . [continues].

3 S's informational discussion: Sex in family life

1(a) Someone else want to address themselves? What were the patterns of behaviour in your family in regards to these three things?   [T: Tony] [calls on Tony] (T-6) [Teacher, 6 sec]

(b) In my house, they were very strict on the kids, they didn't wanna talk about sex or nothing like that. They did touch each other, express affection.   [B-11] [Boy, 11 sec)

2(a) They would do that.   [T-1]

(b) Yeah. But they wouldn't talk about it with us. We learned it off the street.   [B-6]

3(a) So you're saying that your parents never sat you down and talked to you about sex.   [T-4]

(b) (−) . . . You know, I learned it off the street.   [B-7]

4(a) OK, we'll talk about that. That's another question – What did you learn about sex off the street? – What about nudity?   [T-6]

(b) That was nothing, like – ah, you know . . . (−).   [B-12]

5(a) That was sort of natural.   [T-1]

(b) NO RESPONSE (7 sec) [T: Larry]   [X-7]

(c) Are you talking about when we were kids?   [B-1]

6(a) Or even today, though. It's safer to talk about ten years ago, you know.   [T-4]

(b) Because – well, what was it?   [B-5]

7(a) Nudity, talk about sex, and physical affection.   [T-7]

(b) Yeah, talking about sex, that was – it was there, but it was controlled.   [B-6]

8(a) Controlled?   [T-1]

(b) I mean, it was kinda, you know, like – it wasn't like now, you know, when you couldn't even mention anything about sex. It wasn't like that.   [B-9]

9(a) It wasn't that strict.   [T-1]

(b) Because my cousin would make jokes and all that . . . (−) . . . Like I was saying, it was always under control . . . (−) . . . little kids.   [B-13]

10(a) It was more open. Is that what you were saying? Were you saying there was more freedom to talk about it the older you got?   [T-7]

(b) No, it's just what we talked about.   [B-3]

11(a) The kinds of things you talked about.   [T-2]

(b) Yeah . . .   [B-3]

12(a) What about affection?   [T-1]

(b) Yeah. I mean, it's not like I'd see my folks naked on the couch, no . . . [laughter]   [B-9]

13(a) Right. So, quickly, one problem I know I have when I think about this question, I can't ever imagine my parents having sex, or whatever. But the thing is, you know, at least the kids – my parents had 10 kids, so I know they went to bed together at least

10 times, you know . . . [laughter] . . . You know, but I still have this trouble connecting that – the reality. [T-25]

(b) Yeah, I have that trouble, too. I just couldn't – remember I was saying that they showed signs of affection. But . . . (–) . . . children. [T: Right. OK, Marilyn] [B-11]

(c) In our family, you know, we have something like, we sit down and talk about sex . . . (–) . . . to understand it, the way the oldest ones – (G-12) [Girl, 12 sec]

14(a) You all do this together. [T-1]

(b) Yeah, my mother and father and all the rest of us. And just like he said, 'Control'. In a way I understand, because you have to specialize what you mean, you can't use slang, like vulgar language (or street language). Yeah, you can't use that. But you can express, 'What do you mean? What is this?' [G-21]

15(a) So there's a time, you're saying, for questions and answers? [T-3]

(b) Um-hm. [G-1]

16(a) I don't know, you seem to feel good about that. [T-2]

(b) In a way, yes, 'cause . . . (–) . . . [T: Larry] [G-11]

(c) That's – something like that I think is good, too, because it makes for more openness amongst members of the family also, in a sense, you know . . . (–). [B-10]

17(a) Helps to tie it up . . . [Laughter] . . . [T: John] [T-1]

(b) My parents talked . . . [T: Talk louder] . . . They talked to me about this, you know. They'd discuss about sex and all that. But I feel like – a lot of times I feel uncomfortable talking about sex. I know that . . . (–) . . . takes place . . . [laughter] [B-23]

18(a) You're saying they're willing to talk to you, though. [T-2]

(b) Right. [B-1]

(c) See, and in my case, what they're telling me, I know something that they don't know. Because, they have . . . (–) . . . and you look at them seriously and all that . . . (–) . . . And I want to get their attention. 'Cause if I try to correct her, she doesn't believe me. [B-20]

19(a) She won't listen. [T-1]

(b) Right. So I feel, I get angry with her, you know. [B-5]

20(a) So, even though she's willing to talk about it, it still sounds strained, right? [T: Jackie] [T-4]

(b) (–) . . . talk about sex . . . (–) . . . [T: Among yourselves] . . . (–) . . . You know what I mean? [T: Name] [G-25]

(c) In my family situation . . . (–) [B-10]

21(a) Like you were saying, you learn a lot from your older brothers and sisters. [T: Alvin, are you agreeing? OK, Shawn]   [T-4]

(b) One thing I don't understand, you know, like in my family, even though my mother – I know my father is different – but my mother and my sister are all real close, you know. I mean, talking about sex is nothing in my house.   [G-17]

22(a) Pardon me, Shawn . . . [MESSENGER INTERRUPTION] . . . OK, I'm sorry for that, Shawn. Hey, let's settle down. I'm sorry for that interruption.   [T-19]

(b) That's OK. I don't understand why . . . (–) . . . talk about. My mother talked about it like talking about going to a dance or something . . . [T: Like the weather] . . . It's no big deal . . . [T: Right] . . . I mean, I can remember she telling me about sex when I was about 8 years old.   [G-16]

23(a) How did you react as an 8-year-old?   [T-2]

(b) I think I was curious, you know.   [G-3]

24(a) Did you ask her?   [T-1]

(b) I think I used to ask her questions. And my mother, she says, 'Look . . .', she said, she rather for me to ask her than ask somebody off the street. Because she said, now if I come home pregnant, she said, 'I told you so'. I mean . . . [laughter]   [G-12]

(c) My mother – it's no big deal. I'll go home and talk about it tonight, you know.   [G-5]

25(a) You talk with her about the class?   [T-1]

(b) Oh, yeah, all the time.   [G-2]

26(a) What did she say?   [T-1]

(b) She didn't say nothing. She just say, 'Oh, yeah?' . . . [laughter] . . . [T: Sharee]   [G-3]

(c) Like, in my house there's not too much talk about it. Like, if you bring it up, you know, like my father, he'll go back into the . . . (–) . . . You know, and stuff like that. He'd never bring it up. When they did bring it up to me, I didn't hardly know about it, so I just sat there and listened . . . [laughter]   [G-26]

27(a) So you're saying that your dad goes off on these tangents, talking . . . what? . . . telling stories, or . . .   [T-7]

(b) Yeah, or . . . (–).   [G-11]

28(a) OK, so you're saying they're not so willing to listen or hear your story.   [T-3]

(b) Well, my mother, she like, she's sort of open, she realizes that she can't go back . . . (–) . . . everything. So she's real different from my father . . . (–) . . . [T: Shan]   [G-17]

(c) It's just like sort of . . . [T: Speak up] . . . Just like, sort of like Shawn . . . (–) . . . When I was young . . . (–) . . . hospital, OK?

... (–) ... So I was pregnant, OK? ... (–) ... They told me, 'To get circumcized'. And I said, 'What's circumsized?' ... [laughter] ... You know, I was real, awful young, you know? ... (–) ... She said, 'OK, sit down', so we talked about it, you know? ... (–) ... We talk about it ... (–) ... We don't have no certain time. [G-66]

29(a) It's not a traumatic event. [T-1]

(b) It becomes a little bit lighter, that's what I want to say. [G-3]

30(a) Let's go on to the last topic.

4 W's dialectical discussion: Parent–child relations

1(a) I don't think they're totally incompatible, the things you're saying. I just think there are two different ways of looking at them. OK? I mean, I think when you say that you're being led to really kinda make your own way more, I think that's a response to that you really are being influenced by a lot of forces beyond – you have to respond to a lot of things beyond your family, beyond the small society. You know? And I think that's what he was saying, that in the past we tended to be limited in those sorts of situations, whereas now we really do need to go beyond our family, to be able to deal with those situations, those influences for growing earlier on, maybe. Does that fit, do you think? OK, good ... [T: Regina] [calls on Regina] [T-46] [Teacher, 46 sec]

(b) I don't see what Paul and Steve said as two separate ideas. I think that both of them approve of the way things have happened in the past and the future. And that's why I said that in the past, you know, I think that our generation was led to believe that, well, the teenagers, they were young adults, like. The parents were very strict on them. At that point, I remember my father telling me that people were never allowed to contradict their parents, whatever they say, it was accepted, and you weren't able to ask or even think on your own to see if it fit. And I think that, well, I do think that they had a little bit more respect for not only their elders but their peers, too. You know what I mean? ... (um-hm) ... And like today, I feel as though we've made some improvement, but we still like, slip back in a slump because, well now our communication is more open, we are able to question, you know, what our parents say, and disagree with it, and everything like that. I'm not saying that it'll work, but you know we can bring it up, not that we're backed down. And we have – even though we improved it that way, we still, we don't have as much respect as for other people or our friends. So I don't look at it as a separate idea, I think both of them are, you know, a combination.   [G-83] [Girl, 83 sec]

2(a) All right, in a way you're taking it in a different element, you know, I think more kinda personal relationships . . . (–) . . . for one another. But not in the . . . (–) . . . case, because you're saying that there's more – could I ask you why do you think – I mean, I would presume that you think it is good that there is some more opportunity for young people to really voice their own opinion. Why do you think that's important, or necessary, now?   [T-32]

 (b) I think so because, well, in that way, as being taught something, you understand it. There's a difference in being told to do something, understanding it, and being told to do something and doing it because you're afraid of what might happen if you don't. And I feel as though my parents, they were told to do different things then, certain situations were good for them, because this was their parents talking to them, you know, and they weren't going to defy them. Well, if I have another way of thinking, and my mother or father told me to do something, I'm going to question them. Even if I end up doing it, or if I don't, I still have the priority to question, to think through it.   [G-39]

3(a) Good, OK, good. I think that's, you know, a really clear analysis. Do you feel that – do your parents themselves even agree that they think maybe it's better that you be able to really question them at times?   [T-16]

 (b) In my family situation?   [G-1]

4(a) Well, yeah, our parents in general, if you want.   [T-3]

 (b) It's kinda difficult, because my mother seems to be more of a liberal, I guess you would say, and she goes along with me more and I learn an awful lot from her. But my father – and I can't blame him for it – is like, he can only do what he's been taught. And from his parents I know some things I can't say to him, a lot of things I can't question him on. He's more a 'I said it, you do it'.   [G-23]

5(a) OK, good. That's a really good illustration there . . . [T: Steve]   [T-4]

 (b) I agree with her almost all the way up until the end, where she said it should be partly a responsibility of ours. I think the parent should have – there's not enough respect, is what I was trying to say. I feel it should be back the other way. The other way you don't figure out – you lose respect for the parents, let's see, by – you question them. The other way, if you don't question them, you always have somebody to look up to for one answer . . . [T:

All right. Anna] . . .   [B-30] [Boy, 30 sec]

(c) (–) . . . But I wasn't arguing with (father) . . . [laughter] . . . (–) . . . And he said, 'No'. And I just wanted to know why, you know, what he thought. And he started yelling at me, like, why am I arguing with him? 'I'm not arguing with you, father, I really want to know why.' . . . (–)   [G-50]

6(a) How do you mean?   [T-1]

(b) I was wondering 'why?' . . . (–) . . . It's OK, that's human nature.   [G-7]

7(a) OK, yeah, I mean I don't think that it necessarily is disrespectful. I think it's probably good. I think some people might be just kinda protective. People do try to get into arguments. But – it's human. But there's sometimes people do this want to egg somebody on, to see how they would answer something. But at the same time I think it's legitimate sometimes to just want to know what they think. But that's not like other people do it, so . . . (–) . . . apparently with her father there are certain limits . . . [T: Tommy]   [T-45]

(b) You can have all the respect in the world for your parents, but there's no reason why you shouldn't be able to voice your opinion on what you think is right, if your parents don't agree with you. Or sometimes the only reason for talking like that is you're at the age where you should be able to, like if you don't agree with your parents, ask them why. You're not little kids where you have to snap to do everything that they say.   [B-24]

8(a) All right, how do you maintain the respect? Steve was – you know, that's another problem. Is there a way to really ask for the reasons and that sort of thing without being disrespectful? And where your parents can really maintain their decision as your parents without having to simply say, 'Well, I said so, that's gotta be the way it is' – ? . . . [T: Do you want to talk about that?]   [T-26]

(b) You don't really lose no respect for them by questioning them. If they tell you to do something, you could ask them why you want to do it and they'll tell you. But if they still want you to do it, you still gotta do it no matter what. No matter what the reasons, if they tell you to do it, you gotta do it.   [B-14]

9(a) So in the end, the respect might come from accepting their wisdom, whether you understand it or not, huh?   [T-7]

(b) My parents will say . . . (–).   [B-12]

10(a) OK. And yet, you know, as Regina was saying, in the past it did tend to be more like that, that parents were considered kinda total authorities, and I mean, it seemed like it wasn't a completely impossible situation for people to live like that, for long times. And yet for us, it just doesn't seem quite right if you don't have at least the opportunity to hear the reasons why your parents do what they do, or . . .   [T-32]

(b) (–) . . . (OK. Chris)   [S-4]

(c) (–) . . . our family has respect and all that kind of thing. When my parents ask us to do something, like housework, there's no question, because you know housework has to be done. Well, if it does come to questioning why do they do things they do, you're free . . . [P.A. BELL] . . . Both my parents, they didn't have, when they were children, they didn't have the strict parents, 'you have to do this, that's it'. My mother was in the hospital all her life, my father was in an orphanage. They never had the strict parents. So when it came to us, we were just like, they treated us as little people . . . (–) . . . I dunno, there was always respect. And yet whenever we wanted it . . . (–) . . . you know, they like to hear what we didn't understand . . . [T: OK, good. Tommy]   [G-66]

(d) Like, most parents when they say, 'Don't question whatever I say', I think that's a cop-out, because there could be fault in what they're saying and they don't want you to find fault because they want the human authority . . . [T: OK. Regina]   [B-17]

(e) I think he has a point of view or whatever, but I think, taking from what Chris said, that that shows the point of view that parents are human too. And they relate to situations only from what they have been taught. And the way Chris' parents were brought up, it's easy for them to relate to her and understand her feelings, because it sounds like a situation they were in, they probably, you know, had a lot of care and understanding given to them. And just like – I don't know what his name is – but just like he said, some parents are 'Listen to what I say, and you have to do what I say', and everything – this is because that's the kind of atmosphere they were brought up in when they were children. And if you just keep on harping at your parents, what else they going to do? They've been living like that for – what? – 30–40 some odd years. You can't bring them up all over again. So, like it's a situation you have to bear with. You have to try and deal with it on your own.   [G-60]

11 (a) All right. I think this is really a good illustration of how the family, let's say, really shows the differences partly just in historical development.

5 P's problematical discussion: Multiple personality

10(a) So, Eve White the quiet introvert, was the most dominant. OK, now we're back to the question. We're trying to solve, with the little bit of psychology that we have – we know it's dysfunctional to have three personalities – we want to help this woman to have one personality. How – what might we do? . . . [T: Gabriella] [calls on Gabriella] [T-21] [Teacher, 21 sec]

(b) I think that you could try to, ah, get Eve White to see herself as Eve Black, and ah, once she sees herself like this, then, whatever's causing this, split personality, she might try and deal with both of them, and make both one personality, and change it. Because, I wouldn't knock them out, I would combine them. [G-28] [Girl, 28 sec]

11(a) Do you think there'd be an advantage of knocking them out? [T-3]

(b) Yeah, if you knocked both out. [G-4]

12(a) If you knocked Eve White and Eve Black out, and left Jane? [T-4]

(b) Well, aren't Eve White and Eve Black Jane? [B-3] [Boy, 3 sec]

(c) (–) [S-3]

13(a) What would be the danger of that? Why not, as one solution, why not destroy the first two – if you had the psychological tools – and leave Jane? [T-11]

(b) That's what we want to do. [G-5]

14(a) That's what you want to do? [T-1]

(b) That's why I'd combine them, you know – Eve Black and Eve White. But you can't do that. [G-6]

15(a) Well, supposing you have the tools? In other words, supposing you have the psychological know-how to knock out two personalities. Now, from what you know, is that a good idea? [T-9]

(b) Yeah, I think so/I don't think so . . . [T: Duane] [S-3]

(c) Wouldn't she gain another personality? . . . [T: Say that again] . . . Wouldn't she gain another personality? [B-9]

16(a) How do you know – that's a good question – how do you know she wouldn't gain another personality? You got rid of Black and White; you got Jane left; how do you know she wouldn't get another one? [T-11]

(b) (–) . . . [T: Mitchell] [S-3]

(c) I said, how do you know that the two that you knocked out, and the one that you left, are suitable? – the one that's left is – the original one? [B-9]

17(a) I don't know . . . [T: Yvonne]   [T-3]

   (b) OK, now, first I would – if I was the psychiatrist, I would go all the way back to her childhood. And I'd find out from her how she was – not from her but, you know, through other sources – ask them exactly how was she as a child, even when she was one or two years old, because it did say that, in the book, that her split personality started as far back as a child. I mean, as far back as when she was a child, she used to do, you know – get into different things. Then I would – I wouldn't knock out . . .   [G-42]

18(a) Stop there for a moment, Yvonne. Supposing you take this approach – what do you expect to find? If you have a grown woman winding up in your office with three personalities – what do you expect to find back there in her childhood?   [T-16]

   (b) Something that could have flared up or something.   [G-4]

19(a) Like what?   [T-1]

   (b) I don't know! That's what we're looking for!   [G-3]

20(a) OK, come on, let's find it! [T: Mike]   [T-2]

   (b) You'd probably expect to find problems she had at home, you know – like mistreatment from her parents.   [B-7]

21(a) How would that . . .   [T-1]

   (b) 'Cause, ah, like it set up, like, insecurity – and she might look for something else inside herself to compensate for that, so she developed a new personality . . . [T: OK. Darryl]   [B-12]

   (c) OK, like getting back to the childhood thing – like see who her idols were. See where the person had her idols.   [B-12]

22(a) OK, but how would that – if you found out who her heroes or her idols were, what would that have to do with splitting off into two personalities? . . . [T: Terrence]   [T-9]

   (b) Wouldn't you want to try and be like your idol? You know, if you were idolized, you know, you were more or less one of the big idols, to a certain point. Then like, ah, she had an auntie that was shot, and you know, she admired her for the way she was – maybe she'd be shot down as long as she's like her auntie. She'll go home and see that her mother is a nice housewife. She'd want to be like that. Or somebody else – her friends – something like that.   [B-35]

23(a) We all experience what you just said! How come – so it – don't we? . . . [T: Yeah] . . . How come she wound up in such a, such a dump?   [T-11]

   (b) Well, wouldn't that be some kind of restrictions in her background that wouldn't allow her to do that, such as her parents not letting her do something, to the point that she had to, like, ah . . . [G-14]

24(a) Did you see the movie? [T-1]

(b) No. [G-1]

25(a) No. OK, something like that is suggested in the movie – that the trauma was so great that it caused the creation of a new personality . . . [T: Duane] [T-10]

(b) It could be like – you want to do something like that . . . (–) . . . go with the stronger personality . . . (–) . . . a person, you know, like is reading a lot of books and stuff like that . . . (–) . . . 'I want to be just like her'. [B-26]

26(a) OK, I think you'd have to put that together with trauma. That kind of idea, that several of you have expressed, put that together with trauma. In other words, if you try to imitate as a little child, your idols, and you were severely punished for it – this is just one general example – then, for whatever reasons, you might be forced to split in two. I think that's the only way I can put it together – it's been a long time since I read that . . . [T: Yvonne] [T-33]

(b) OK. Isn't it true that whatever your conscious mind turns out, your subconscious reacts, don't it, right? Now, say she's saying to herself – she's getting it in her mind that she wants to be just like that lady, and her subconscious mind's gonna pick up on that and react on that, and she's gonna start acting like a certain person, doing the same kind of things that certain persons do, you know – she's gonna pick up that personality, act that person. [G-37]

27(a) You're working – we're working on one model now, aren't we? We're working on the idol model. I wonder if there are others . . . [T: Mike] [T-10]

(b) There's got to be others, 'cause you can have a personality that you develop under, you know, constant conflict. Like a child might be exposed to two opposites and it's always rehearsing, it's always going on, over and over and over again. OK? The child might be split into each one of those worlds, in order to deal with it. [B-22]

28(a) OK, good. That wasn't in the book, either. If there's so much conflict – if there's so much conflict, you might have to shift gears without even knowing it, just to protect the self – is the model that he's using, the conflict model . . . [T: Anthony] [T-15]

(b) What about like, an overprotective parent and stuff? Like, you can be very shy and things like that. Any maybe she had parents that told her, you know, that she shouldn't go out with no guys, or nothing like that . . . (–) . . . that wasn't the kind of person she was. She was a little more outgoing. And maybe when she was young and that, maybe that . . . (–) . . . her parents had a real overpowering effect on her. That could change her.   [B-31]

29(a) OK, how many of you read *I Never Promised You a Rose Garden* – Hannah Green's book?

NAME INDEX

SUBJECT INDEX